I0479677

Instagram Marketing

The Perfect Guide for Beginners Who Want To Make a Difference and Increase Business Revenues with Tips and Secrets to Easily Build a Strong Follower Base.

Author Name: Harvey Quick

Description

Have you ever wondered how Instagram came to be or how you can use it to your advantage? This book is the answer you need! You will learn so much that you can use to your advantage with this book that you will be able to achieve your Instagram goals while making sure that you have got the best information possible to make sure, that you will be able to take your Instagram to the next level. Many people who download this app just think that you download a pretty picture and that is it. In reality, it is so much more than that and there is so much more involved in the process that you need to be aware of. Being aware of this is going to give you a better understanding of what it is you need to do to help you achieve your goals.

The book will tell you everything you need to know about how to gain and keep followers while ensuring that you have the ability to turn your followers into making dollars. This is going to be a great way for you to begin to turn yourself into an influencer or making your business skyrocket to the next level by making a business profile that will make customers flock to you. This is such an important thing for people to understand because it is one thing to be able to gain followers but quite another to be able to keep them interested and following you for good instead of coming to you and then leaving. With the features, that Instagram offers you as both a person who wants to gain popularity through this social media platform or being able to utilize the millions of people that use this app to your advantage through your pictures and content for your profile. With so many users on the app, there are so many opportunities for you here no matter what it is you would like to do or utilize this app for.

There are many things that you will need to consider when making Instagram work for you. How will you find your niche? How can you make your followers love you and want to stay with you? How do find followers in the first place or let them find you? How do you grow a following large enough to be an influencer? How can you take your business further by using your Instagram for your benefit? All of these questions and more are answered in this book and you will be able to use Instagram to take you to a place where you have thousands of followers instead of just family and friends. You can even connect with famous authors, celebrities and companies that can take you beyond where you thought you could go!

By buying this book, you will be an Instagram pro in no time! Learn all the tricks and tips you need with this book and learn how to push past everyone who does not know how to use this to their advantage. Come learn the secrets and become a top influencer!

Table of contents:

Chapter one: The History Of Instagram

Instagram has become one of the biggest and most recognized social media outlets. It is a great way for friends to interact with each other and they can see hundreds of different ideas and pictures of things they are interested in. It also lets you see hundreds of different videos. A great benefit of the ability to do this with pictures and videos is that they are on any subject and can be really insightful or helpful to you. A great example of what we mean here is that if you are into fitness and health and you see a picture of a healthy meal. The person who posted the picture more than likely will post the recipe, this, in turn, helps you get healthy. Someone else could post a video that could give you an insight into your life or a business idea. It is very easy to get inspired by Instagram.

This platform is said to be a success right from the start and many people want to utilize what this platform can offer them. This platform was developed in the beautiful city of San Francisco California by two men. The two men that created the Instagram app decided that the app they were trying to make, unfortunately already looked like other apps that were on the market and they obviously wanted to make it different so it would stand out and not get lost among the others. In order to do this, they wanted to focus only on communication through images. Therefore, they took out all of the features from the extra features so that the only thing that the app has now is the ability to upload photos and the ability to like and comment on them as well. They renamed it Instagram and marketed it as a way to send a telegram instantly.

It launched nine years ago and it grew right away and gained over one hundred thousand people using it in a single week! In just seven days, the numbers had skyrocketed like crazy. From this point, it was able to reach the mark of a million in less than three months. This app began taking a phenomenal leap in people using it because they loved the new way they could share with their friends and families. Instagram only took two months to build but there was more than a year of work that went behind it to make it what it was. It was later bought by Facebook. Facebook is another huge social media platform that people use and it does so much. Today the Instagram app can boast that it has over five hundred million users, but amazingly, those numbers are still growing and they are getting more and more every day!

The really unique thing about Instagram is that it is compared to when humans first came to the Earth. When we used to communicate with each other, we would draw pictures to be able to show each other what we meant. We would also draw pictures so that people would remember us forever and we could express how we feel. This is like Instagram. We take pictures to show what feeling, doing was, or what we want to share with others. There is also a love for people to watch other people's lives and adventures and this is a way to do this and feel closer to people as well.

The first photo that was ever put on this app was of the creator's dog. It was an adorable photo of course because who does not love puppies? When the app began to get more attention, it was then that the investors began to take interest and they wanted a piece of this as well. By raising over six million dollars from many various investors, they were able to gain the attention of two bigger fish. They gained the attention of two major social media platforms. Facebook, and Twitter. Twitter is a platform where people can express their opinions, follow celebrities, upload photos and more. It is a great platform to utilize. These two platforms would give them the ability to hire a lot of people, but they chose to keep using a few. They declined the offer from Twitter because they wanted to make sure that they remained independent. This was very important to them and it was something that they did not have to compromise on because they got another offer after this one.

When they got their next offer it was an offer from Facebook, and they decided to go with it because Facebook offered what Twitter had not offered. Facebook offered the creators the ability to be able to keep Instagram independently managed. This happened after just two years after Instagram was launched and the creators of Instagram accepted. In that same year, they brought in over twenty different languages along with a new filter to the app and people were loving the new improvements. Only another year after that they introduced the ability to introduce videos and tagging pictures along with the other features that this app is known for.

The interesting thing is that this app became famous practically overnight. There are many reasons that are believed to be that they are so successful. Some of the following reasons it is believed to be so successful are the list below.

- It is a free app and everyone loves free!
- You can make a business profile, which will attract new people to you.
- You can become an influencer (both of these two tips are ways to earn a lot of money).
- No ads like other platforms, so no frustration. This makes it so much fun to use. Ads are annoying and they interrupt what you are looking at.
- It has amazing features that are really fun and it updates daily to suit your needs.
- People love watching videos and looking at pictures so this is what Instagram does for you.

They can take normal photos and can turn them into really amazing memories.

Instagram has become so popular that it has launched shows that people rewatch repeatedly for tips. It has also launched thousands of blogs and it has also launched hundreds of different posts on blogs around the world on how to gain followers on Instagram. There have been just as many on how to earn money from your Instagram posts, pictures or content that you are posting.

It is really an amazing thing to be able to have so many benefits that you can receive from Instagram and how you can find the best way to gain your audience. This book will give you every hint that you need and every tip that you need to make sure they are using Instagram to its best potential and that you can gain great benefits from it as well.

The history of Instagram is quite compelling when you think about it because it was made from two men who had an idea for an app that would be able to make people happy and it not only worked but it blew past others in the same field because it offered a new twist that others didn't. This ability to set it apart was why it skyrocketed to fame. Today so many people have happiness by this and they have found a way to share their stories with others, inspire people, and give themselves amazing opportunities.

Chapter two: Choosing Your Name

In this chapter, we are going to deal with choosing the right Instagram name for your account. Choosing the right Instagram name is going to be able to help you get those followers that you need and increase your popularity, which is also what you, want. Social networks are booming and they have so many more users than they ever did before so it is really challenging to be able to find a name that stands out but is something that you like and is going to attract users at the same time. There are a lot of difficulties that you might face when you are trying to choose the name, such as the name, that you choose may have already been taken or you may have to spell it differently than you want to. You also need, in some cases, to add strange symbols, those can be really difficult to remember, and it can also be really difficult for your followers to remember as well. As such, this might not be the best solution for you, but there are plenty of names out there that could also be like yours and this can also leave the confusion among the people that you want to follow you as well. If your name sounds too much like somebody else's, those people are going to go to that other person thinking that they found someone they wanted or got then confused with you. If they thought, they were trying to follow someone else and then it turned out that they were not actually looking for you they could unfollow. On the other hand, to this though, they might decide to stay with you because they like your content even if they were not meaning to find you.

You should be aware that your Instagram name is a really important factor because it is the first thing that they are going to see besides your bio and it is going to come across to users as a good name or a bad name. Therefore, it is either going to captive them or make them not want to follow you. Pay attention to the following tips that we are going to be giving you in this chapter to avoid mistakes.

The first thing that you should do is consider the type of account that you are wanting to create and then the name for your profile. A great example of this is there are personal brand accounts or a personal account. A business account or an account about life and entertainment things of that nature. A great example is to look at the book of people on Instagram. Book love is a serious thing that is coming back and everyone wants to be that book nerd or have that bookstagram. So as such, there are so many people that have really good names and creativity so that you can find them and they all have to do with books. Each name has something to do with their love of books and they want to stand out so that you can find them. Their accounts are also very creative and they are engaging as well to get you to stay with them over everyone else.

Therefore, the first thing that you are going to have to do is set up your Instagram account. If you already have one, then you do not have to worry about this because you already have an account and so you already had your username in place. What you are going to need to do is build your profile so you will have to put your full name, your username, password, and a photo. Now, remember what you are going to put your username as is how people are going to find you. The name that you choose for your Instagram page is going to be vital. Your Instagram name is going to be what people use to see you so think about it as a website. There are thousands of websites on the internet but you have your favorites that stick outright? They have done something to make you recognize them and not other people. When people search for you, it is your name that is going to need to be recognizable and it is going to need to be something that pops right away. The way that you are making your name is going to be what determines a significant amount of your success on Instagram. Chances are that you are not already a famous celebrity that everybody knows or a famous company and brand that is monetized all over the world that everybody knows. The chances are you are just someone who is just starting out and you want people to notice you and notice your brand. Therefore, what you need to do is maximize your growth on Instagram and the first way to do that is to choose the right name.

Remember that people will be disappointed if they cannot see content that matches your name or they are going to be confused because they are not going to see the correlation between the two. A great example of what we mean here is if you are a vegan. If you are a vegan and you are posting content about eating cheeseburgers or eating a steak, this is going to make your followers not like you because they're going to see that not only are you not doing what your name implies but you're going completely against what your name implies. Another way that this will confuse your fans is they would think 'why are you eating meat if you are a vegan'? This is a very simple and a bit of an obvious example but it can really help you see what we mean. Another example that we could state is if you are a woman who claims that she will never wear luxury items and you are spotted with a Gucci handbag your fans will know you lied. This is not what they want. They want someone who is real and not pretending. There are a lot of fake profiles on social media already. Focus on being real and true to yourself instead. Things like that are really, what is going to make a difference. It sounds like common sense but many people will just jump into this process before they think about it and then it is harder for them to get started.

Here is a trick to consider. There are over seven hundred million people that use Instagram and chances are, your name is already taken. So let us work around it. This is what we mean. Think of keywords like inspiration, or wanderer, traveler, and things that are like that. If you use the words alone, they are taken. If you try to use them together such as inspirational wanderer, or travel inspiration, things that are like that will give you a better chance to make sure that it is not taken. Choosing two complementary 'buzz' words gives you a much higher chance of finding something that has not been taken, but you still have the chance to have SEO optimization. SEO means search engine optimization and what this means is that when you type a word into Google, it will find you simply and easily and you appear at the top of the list instead of on-page five or six of the results.

Think about the content you are going to post and have your name have to do with that content. Like we said above the name and content need to go together well and not be confusing but to be concise and clear so that you do not confuse your fans and followers. A great way to help you decide on your name is to write a list of buzzwords that have to do with the type of content you will be posting. Let us say that you are going to have a bookstagram. For this, you will want to write words that have to do with books. Such as the following examples.

- Library
- Reading
- Books
- Fantasy
- Romance

See these little buzz words would show up really well on a Google search. This is what is going to help you get seen and found. Make a list of about ten or fifteen words. Then you can choose. You can also choose alliteration and this is a great thing to use for your name as well. Let us say that your name is Tony and you want you are wanting your account to be about traveling and seeing the world and beautiful sights. You could name yourself TravelingTony. The alliteration is clear and concise which means it is easy to find you and it is easy to say. If you choose not to do this that is fine too. Another tip is to try an adjective with the buzzword. For this example, we are going to take you back to the book lover. So let us say that you are a fan of the old-time libraries and the beauty of what they can create. A house for thousands of stories and pages for you to learn and explore.

You can use some great adjectives here to make that name stand out. Think carefully about some great adjectives here. You could name yourself moving library since you are traveling to different places to find them each time, you could go with walking library to give the illusion that they move around as you do, there are many different things that you could go with here to make your name stand out so strongly that no one will be able to forget it.

Choosing a surprise word to make yourself seen can work great for you as well. Think about your niche and use words that would go with that. When you think of traveling, you might not be thinking about seasons but this could be a cool idea to get you noticed. You can call yourself the seasonal traveler or something that has to do with that title or you could think about the word barefoot. In today's society, the word barefoot means that your free and your moving and making sure that your ability to be in a sense or have any sort of idea about oneness with yourself. When you are traveling, you can make this work for you. You could say something like a barefoot traveler, or barefoot wanderer, there are many different ways you can go with this and make your name be better.

Originality is important because it is going to make a huge difference on your account and you need to avoid a brand name in your name as well particularly if you are not a member of that brand. If you want to look like your part of a community or brand, make your own brand and remember that brand names can get lost in the crowd. Rhyming can help you get into the right mode as well because they are funny while being cute and fun and they can really help you get noticed and bring people to you.

Other easy tips that can help with your name are to add I am in front of it so that they know it's the real you and so that you can let them know that your the one they are trying to find. Another great thing you can do is get your account verified although this is something that most celebrities do because they are more well known than others are.

Instagram has a checker to see what is available and what is not and there is no limit to how many times you can try. Get creative and use what feels good to you and your heart. If all else doesn't work and you end up choosing a name that you later hate, you can fix this and change the name without losing the followers you already have but it can cause issues for those that want to follow you. Particularly if you have chosen to connect all of your accounts or you have the same username on your other accounts. You will have to change all of them if you do this and some do not give you the option to do that.

If you are still having issues with coming up with a name for yourself you can be frustrated and this an issue with you. This is not an easy thing to do because it is a complicated thing for a lot of people and that is alright. If this is true for you, you can use what is known as a name generator. There are plenty of online tools that you can use for free. You will be able to use these to help you come up with ideas for a name for yourself. The only thing that you will have to do is plug in a few keywords and it will give your ideas for what you should do for your name.

This next tip is actually kind of fun and you will be able to think of something unique. Think of celebrity couples. You play with their names and give them a cute name as a couple, right? Think of Ben and Jennifer. They began to call them Bennifer. This is a combo of their names. The same thing with a famous model that was on a famous show. Her name was Melissa Rose and she shortened it to Melrose. In a later season on the show, one of the models said they respected her idea and did the same. She shortened her name from Whitney Michelle to Whittelle. You can do this with your name too! Let us say your name is Christopher Lewis. Put it together and your username can be Crewis. Interesting and fun, it would not be the sort of thing you would see every day. Another trick with your name is to rearrange your name. This is different than what we have just said above. Think about it like this. If your last name is Stan, you could change the letters around and play with it to find something you like. Maybe you could change it to tans or another word from the four letters.

You can also reference your location for something that is a little different, you can remember that your name can have to go with what your brand is, and you can use clues and words that tie into your personal brand and what you are trying to achieve. You can also use your title. Think about a famous doctor or celebrities. They have a title that sets them apart and it helps people find them and recognize them so that they can have more people know who they are.

Look up keywords to try to find something that appeals to you and what you are trying to achieve. If you notice that the keywords your typing in have a lot of results and followers, you've just walked into a highly competitive field. Just remember that you need to be creative. Remember also, to keep it simple. Instagram gives you thirty characters for your username. Nevertheless, that does not mean that you should pack it full of symbols, letters and other things because it is going to be an overly complicated potential mess.

You do not need to be a perfectionist but you do want to take a good amount of time to come up with the right name. Ask people you trust because they are going, to be honest with you and there are other things that you need to consider as well like pronunciation it should be easy to say whatever your name is going to be but it should also be unique because you do not want something that is already taken. You want to avoid similarities to other people and you do not want to experience copyright infringement because either this is a serious pain to have to deal with or it can be costly as well. The length should not be too long because the longer it is, the harder it was going to pronounce and all it does is add confusion to people who do not understand what your page is all about as we have said before.

Symbols in your name to make it unique is something that ideally you want to avoid using at all but that might not be realistic considering the vast amount of people that are on Instagram. Try to limit your use of these though and never put two or more periods or symbols in the same name or right beside each other.

The reason for this is that it makes it harder for people to search for you and it makes it harder for people to find you. You should also keep ethnicity and religion along with other things like gender out of your name as well. If you have these in your name, it is going to limit the potential size of your audience before you even begin. You need to respect what your followers want to see if you want to keep them around. Engage with your content on your Instagram page. As we said before your name needs to be relevant to what you are posting.

Using your niche as a keyword in the first part of your name can help as well. Enter the mind of the person who was searching for your niche and what the first thing that they are going to type in the search field is. That keyword. If it is not, then your name could get lost among the other search results. This is a really simple way to utilize search engine optimization within the app. Try to keep popular names out of your name as well there are several huge Instagram accounts that dominate those niches already and you're going to be facing a very hard uphill climb if you attempt to do that. A unique name will make your page much easier to discover when people are searching for you and you can build yourself up in your own way. Another great tip is to make sure that your name is on different social media platforms and while we mention this above there is another thing to think about when doing this. Therefore, what we mean is if you choose a name on your Instagram and you have that name on your other accounts as well, this is going to ensure that your brand is simplified and unified. The only exception to this would be if you wanted to keep your personal account separate from the account to use for business and influencing. Obviously if you don't want people to find your family or your friends and you want to keep your personal life separate, then you could create a different account with that same name for your fans to see and they wouldn't be able to see your family or friends and this is okay because many people want to keep their private life private. With the issues going on in today's society that's honestly a very good idea to keep your private life private and separate because this eliminates the potential chance of stalkers and other problems.

If you have a website then you should have the name be very similar to your Instagram name. You do not need to spend a lot of money to make your own website and honestly, if you are just starting out a website might not be the best option for you because it takes a lot of time. However, if you are going to go this route because of the opportunities that a website will afford you then make sure the names are similar so that they can find you easier or make them exactly the same if the website allows you to do this. In certain cases, they do not allow you to do this so just be aware that that might be an issue.

By understanding the tips that we have given you in this chapter you should be able to come up with a name for your Instagram account that will be engaging, fresh and cool while making sure that you have the option to be unique and you will be able to gain followers. Once you gain those followers, you will be able to let you keep those followers because they will be able to find you through the keywords that you have used. You will also be able to take your Instagram to the next level, which is what we are trying to achieve here. The name is the first thing and now that we have covered it, we will be showing you how to find your best niche. This is a very important part of Instagram and as such, we will be giving you all the information about your niche and how to choose the best one possible for you.

Chapter three: How You Find Your Best Niche

One of the biggest things that you need to do for Instagram is to find your niche. A niche is what is known as a suitable position in either your employment or your life or a comfortable position in either one. An example of this in an ecological sense would be if a spider is a predator that hunts and a tree that is growing to dominate a canopy then the spider would play the role to serve to be an ecological niche. This is because the garden spider is comfortable with its position. In the business world, a niche would be known as a profitable segment of a particular market that is suitable for your attention. You can identify a niche very simple and there are many different types and tricks that you can use to find out what is the right niche for you in the Instagram world. Finding your niche on Instagram is important because you will be able to gain more followers and you will be able to find a target audience that is in the same field that you are wanting to become a part of. For example, if your niche is health and fitness, you will have amassed a group of followers that are trying to get healthy and learn new exercises or recipes. As this is everyone at some point or another, your followers will reach the thousands quickly if you put in the time and effort.

Therefore, now that we have identified what a niche is the next thing that we need to do is to understand the tips on how to find which one is the right one for you and how to use that to your benefit your Instagram. You want to choose one that is going to work with you and give you the most benefit so this is what we are going to help you within this chapter.

When trying to find your niche on Instagram you want to start your brand or business and you want people to be able to find you. This can be complicated, however, because you can try all your hobbies or your passions and still come away sentiments as if you hadn't hit on something that you really want to do or something that you really want to make your page about. Establish what type of strain on yourself to single out the specific suitable thing may lead you to have unneeded frustration or give up when you do not need to. Now you do want to have diligence in selecting a business or your page and you do want to find a niche that you care about, but it's better to try out what you are passionate about than to be a perfectionist and wait so you can experiment with concepts and then enter your market quickly and gain knowledge from your success or learn from your failure if you have any.

Remember that everyone fails at some point in their life and it is okay. This is part of human nature and no one is perfect. This is a problem that many people face on social media. They want to be perfect and no one is. Even if the Instagrams that look perfect re not. They took a lot of work and time to look at the way they do. Instead of chasing perfection just try your best and do the best that you can. The important thing is to learn from your mistakes and then move on. Do not sit and dwell on what went wrong. This will only hurt you and cause you to feel frustrated. If your first business idea or brand idea does not click, remember that you can invariably grab what you have experienced from that attempt and maneuver onward with a fresh idea. The first thing that you should do when trying to find your niche, however, is to identify your interests and your passions. This is going to be able to tell you, which niche is the best one for you and what you should do once you have chosen one for yourself.

This may be a step that you have previously completed but if you have not, then you should produce a checklist of twenty hobbies or passions that you feel that you care about and you should do this so that you will be able to know what it is that you feel that you should focus on. Instagram is not easy and is neither business nor branding. At some point, it is going to try you. If you are engaged in, the field that you do not have a personal interest in the odds of you giving up is going to double. This is notably true if you are doing this for the first time.

You do not need to find a perfect fit. You just need to find something that you are passionate about. If you are passionate about at least some aspect of doing this, you are going to stick with it and you are going to stick with it for much longer. However, if the topic does not grab your attention then you might not be able to find the driver that you need to keep going.

Some things to help you decide what your interests and passions are to ask yourself the following questions.

- Do you subscribe to any magazines?
- What type of books do you like to read?
- In the library, what topics do you want to learn about?
- Do you belong to a club or an organization?
- Is there a certain type of club you would like to belong to if you could?
- How do you like to spend your free time?
- What do you look forward to when you are not doing anything?
- What do you miss when you are not able to do it?

Asking yourself these questions is going to be able to help you determine what it is that you really care about and this will make finding your niche easier.

The next tip that you should utilize is to identify a problem that you are able to solve. With your list of topics and passions that you are trying to understand if you are passionate about or interested in, you need to start narrowing down your options. You are trying to create a profitable brand or a business that is going to succeed. You need to find the problems that your customers are going to be experiencing and then determine whether you can solve them. People will follow you if they feel like you can solve a problem with them. What you should do is research and try to find popular search terms related to the points of the particular field you want to use.

Another good tip is to go and look at the discussions that are taking place in forums with your niche. What kind of problems are people having? What are they looking for and what do you need to do that others cannot do? Then you should have a one-on-one conversation and make sure that you're creating a framework for asking questions that will help you discover what it is that you are looking for and what they are looking for as well as what they need from you.

You should also research your competition because the presence of competition is not always a bad thing. Competition could actually show you what you need to do and how you need to improve, but you will need to do this for research too. Is the competition in your niche offering quality? Are they fake or are they paying people for reviews? Differentiate yourself from that by being real. Produce real content that is high quality instead of low quality and make sure that you have the volume that they do not.

You also need to be able to determine the profitability of the niche that you have chosen so if you have a good idea of what needs you are getting into. Then you will need to determine how much money you have the potential to make. A great idea to do this is to browse the top products in the category that you have chosen for yourself. If you cannot find any offers then that is not a good sign. It might mean that nobody has been able to use this niche for their benefit. However, this can also mean that you are the first person to have this idea and you might be able to succeed where they were not able to succeed if someone had attempted this or had a similar idea. If your search does turn up a good number of products but not an overabundance, then you are in luck. Make a list of the price points so that you will be able to price your own products or your own brand in that manner. Also, keep in mind that you don't have to have a business or brand with a product offering of your own, you can also partner with other people, other advertisers and other influencers in that same niche. This will help you begin to generate commission when you are working with your own unique idea.

Once you are armed with the information that you need to choose a niche the only thing that has left for you to do is to actually test out your idea. A simple way to do this as a set up a landing page, which is what they offer for pre-sales of a product that you are developing or you can set up a page, and only invite certain people to it and this will help as well because it is a test that you can do. Once you do this, you can drive traffic to the page. When you are able to understand that this is really, what you want to do a test run would help because you will find the mistakes. For instance, your messaging could have issues that need fixing, or you have not found the right offer, maybe you do not know how to read the data. Things of that nature. Having knowledge of these things is really going to help you so having a test run would help solve these issues for you.

After you confirm the viability of your niche you should start, developing a full-fledged website to go with your Instagram if that is something that you want to proceed with. This is a good idea because a website will also be able to generate your income and generate more people to follow you. Your website will be able to generate more traffic to your Instagram and vice versa so, people would be able to find you easier as a result.

Another thing that you will have to make sure that you do is to create your profile and make sure that it looks appealing so that people want to follow you in the first place. Knowing your niche is very important but making sure that people will follow you is just as important.

You need to create a good bio that is going to have keywords that have to do with your niche and you can add other profiles to your Instagram if you want them to be able to find you everywhere. Now, remember when you are deciding your niche, you are also going to be deciding who your audience is going to be based on. For example, if your niche is pets then you should find followers who are interested in pets and you can do successful campaigns with those same people. If your niche is crocheting then you are going to need to find Instagrammers who are interested in crochet. Once you have identified who your audience should be you need to remember that you can always find more people and that you should actively be looking for more audience members as well.

Be sure to hashtag related to your niche and do research to find out which hashtags are the best to be used. Finding posts that use hashtags allows you to find individuals that are interested in the subject they are posting about. You may even find Instagram accounts that are dedicated to the very same subject. If you do that then it is very likely that the followers of that account will be interested in your account as well. You can find the most popular hashtags online by using Google or another internet service but hashtags are very useful when you are using Instagram to support and promote your business or your brand. Hashtags will help you find an audience that is interested in your niche and keep those interested in your content to find you. When trying to determine your niche another great idea for helping you find it is to study the profiles of people who have used hashtags that relate to that niche as well. Look at the followers and check out their profiles. See what they are doing right and what they are doing wrong.

Following hashtag and location tags to an event is also a great idea for your niche to develop an audience and to give your ideas for what you want to do with your niche. Do not forget that you also need to interact with your potential audience so that they will follow you and they will bring more people to you.

If you are wanting to use Instagram for influencing then you should be aware that there are many reasons that influencers cannot break through to the next level and we are going to help you get around that. It seems like influencers come out of nowhere and they skyrocket and are able to work with the best brands and people available. While others get very low offers or someone gets paid a very low cost to sell their product. If you are a successful influencer, it definitely has benefits though you just need to be paid what you are worth.

According to Forbes Magazine, an Instagram user with just a hundred thousand followers can make around five thousand dollars for a single post when you are working with a particular brand. Others are such good influencers that if they show up to a certain spot they can get ten thousand dollars just for a picture.

If you are trying to become an influencer then you also need to find your niche. No matter what you are, utilizing your Instagram for a niche will make it easier for you. Find one that suits you and works well with you. Influencers work in every field and some popular categories are the following.

- Travel
- Home
- Lifestyle
- Photography
- Beauty

- Food and drink
- Business
- Entertainment

Your selection will be critical because this is a market where you are going to build your brand. This is why having a niche is going to help you and picking the wrong one could possibly make you fail. You may find yourself on Instagram with a good number of followers or wanting to get a lot of followers and this is what could make the difference.

A very common misconception when you are finding your niche or when you are an influencer is to find an untapped niche so that you can have all the rewards and no one else. This may work but it is few and far between. Competition is a good thing because it means that there is something worth having. Another great tip is that you should find a niche that has a lot of space for growth. You will find out that in just a year some influencers cannot make it because it is too small or because their niche is not growing. To make sure this does not happen to you, you need to find a niche that is expanding so that you can keep reaping the financial rewards and have increased demand in the marketplace.

Loving your topic is not enough either. You have to know your topic really well. Just because you love it and it makes money does not mean it that you should enter it. Now to be clear, we have said that you need to find a niche that you love but to gain attention from your audience you also have to be able to provide value and this comes from knowledge. Think of it like this. If you are in love with photography and you want this to be your niche but you don't know the first thing about how to take a picture, this might not be the right niche for you to go into because your fans are going to want to see that you're knowledgeable about this and you won't be able to give them the information that they need.

You have to choose a niche that you will know very well so that you can provide a disproportionate amount of value compared to everyone else in the marketplace. This will put you over the top when you are an influencer or in a specific niche. You should also remember that once you have them place you need to post consistently and get creative to get people's attention. Instagram is and can be a very crowded place to grow your brand or to be an influencer.

You are also going to have to figure out how to get creative to get people's attention. We will talk about how to engage with your fans and how to turn your followers into dollars in later chapters so we will not dive too much into that here. When you are an influencer, you can also find brands to work with. When you grow your audience to a good number and they are engaged in following you, you should start looking for brands to work with. The first thing that you want to do is to make sure that the people who are looking at you and your profile know that you are open to working with brands also make sure that you are very clearly stating that you are open to discussing sponsorships because this is something that you're going to have to do for your fans. If your being sponsored and you need to tell them. You can also reach out directly to brands, networks, and marketplaces. If these do not sound like it would be a good idea for you, you can also develop relationships with other influencers.

You could even direct messages or collaborate with people on Instagram. Another thing that you should do once you have your niche in place is to develop a marketing strategy and then execute that strategy. Everyone has a goal for what they want to use Instagram for and you should know what your goal is so that you can be able to use it to your advantage. Becoming popular on Instagram can open a lot of doors for you and having specific needs that you can go into is going to have you be put in a viable growth market which in turn will give you more opportunity to get more followers and more opportunity to be seen and heard.

Another thing that will help you once you have your niche is when people are deciding whether or not you are worth following. You can only get about a half a second to impress them so you should make it count. People are more likely to look at your profile through a little grid that they see and then go from there. This makes it easy for them by having a color scheme. You should make a color scheme, therefore, that goes with your niche.

Another tip you can use to your benefit is to make sure that you are posting pictures that have to do with your niche. As we will go into why it's so important to stay on topic in a later chapter we will only say that if you don't post every day then you should make use of the stories and you should post pictures and stories that have to do with what your niche is on with Instagram. A great example that we have used before is if you're vegan and you're posting pictures of things that have nothing to do with veganism or that go against veganism, if you want your niche to be about veganism you're going to need to post things about that specific topic and avoid doing things that will make people stop following you.

If you need some ideas for some profitable niches then you will need to understand what it is that makes a niche success in the first place. You also need to understand how you are going to be monopolizing your Instagram. Ask yourself the following questions.

- Are you going to be having shoutouts to your fans?
- Will you be uploading for other brands?
- Are you going to be selling your own product?
- Are you going to be selling your own brand?
- Are you going to be driving traffic to earn a commission?

All of these things are good things to know because it is going to tell you how you are going to be using your particular niche for your own benefit. If you are not selling a product or brand and you just want to make the Instagram for another reason then shoutouts and driving traffic to you would still be a good idea for your page because you could still earn passive income. When you are trying to grow a profitable Instagram, some other things to consider are the following.

Where will your demographic be located?
What language do they speak? What is the age that you will be targeting?

Having these factors in mind is going to make it much easier for you to sell or promote to your followers and get more followers to follow you as a result.

So now that we talked about some of the different ways that you can be profitable with a niche, let us talk about some of the most profitable niches on Instagram right now. Some of the most profitable Instagram niches right now are the following.

The luxury lifestyle. You will see things such as watches, clothing, jewelry and you will see supercars galore. This is a very profitable niche to look into because everybody and likes a look into the luxurious lifestyle or seeing things that are beautiful. Most users who follow these accounts cannot afford the items that are being shown but they do like looking in and having an idea of what that lifestyle is going to look like. Travel usually falls into this category as well. For luxury travel, people love to see this as well, but there are specific Instagram users that post this type of content and it does differ a little bit from the luxury lifestyle depending on how the content is produced. This is also different from other forms of travel which we will go over later on in this chapter. Another tip that we will give you about going into this niche on Instagram is that you can get a lot of haters. This is because most of the people that post these things tend to be entitled or they tend to be wasteful. An example of this would be the people that you see on the internet putting an iPad above their head because it is raining. It is usually a five hundred dollar device that they are treating horribly and not caring that is being destroyed because they have the ability to buy another one or five. For people who cannot afford these items, they tend to get very upset that people are showing no respect for their luxurious goods. As such, this is another thing to be aware of.

Another profitable niche that you could look into is travel. Everyone wants to escape the nine to five schedule. Everyone wants to see the world and almost everybody has a huge case of wanderlust. The way that you get rid of that wanderlust is by traveling. The profitable Instagram niche, therefore, is traveling. It is harder to get into and this is where people tend to go wrong. To do this you are going essential to establish an Instagram account that is laser-focused to a specific audience in traveling. What this means is if you are a backpacker, then you are going to appeal to backpackers. If you are a business traveler, you are going to appeal to that demographic. If you were a camper then you would appeal to that demographic and so on and so forth. Luxury travel is a different type and should not be categorized with these as a result.

Luxury travel usually includes mass prices a delicacy, anything luxury. That is why we are saying that you have to be aware of who you are marketing to.

Making money online is also another profitable niche that is a great idea to mention. This is because everybody wants to know how to make their financial situation better and accounts that are focusing on improving the financial lives of others have been an amazing niche for profitable content. Examples include things such as saving money tips, how to start a business, marketing tips or even blogging tips.

Fitness and beauty are two top niches to get into as well. Everyone is always looking for nail tips or beauty tips or how to look their best. Makeup looks and hair tricks can appeal to anyone far and wide and as far as fitness goes, everybody is either a fan of CrossFit or ballet. There are many different ways to get your body fit and different recipes that you can use to your benefit. There are so many different ways you can help people and engage them with these two niches.

You can also have a popular niche with relationships and food. These are another two that are very popular and the reason for this for food is because everyone is always looking for recipes and they love beautiful pictures of food. It inspires them and you can get very creative with how you display the food, what you do with the food, and the ingredients you use. There are beautiful pictures on Instagram of even plain food items like toast that can be turned into a visual masterpiece to inspire other people and to engage them.

As far as relationships go everyone is always looking for relationship advice on how to make a relationship better, or how to make their relationship last longer. They want to know how to have a better marriage or how to have better communication. There are literally thousands of things that you could talk about and discuss on your Instagram and this is all going to be able to get people to relate to you and engage with you and feel connected to you because you are helping them solve a problem that they have in their life. You could really help people and for the better with this niche.

It doesn't matter what niche you pick as long as it's something that you want and is something that you know you'll be able to continuously work on to make sure that it's what you're wanting your page to be. Some of these are very easy to get into but they can also be some of the hardest to sell in due to the saturation of the market. They can also be hard to get followers. They should be something to consider for you however because there are thousands of different brands out there and there are new ones coming up every day. This means there is huge potential for you to grow your followers and still make money from one of these brands. Just because the market is saturated, so much does not mean you cannot get in. It just means it is harder.

If you follow the tips in this chapter you should be able to provide yourself not only with a niche that you love but you will be able to use this for your benefit and be able to make money as well as gaining followers as well. All of these things will help your Instagram go further.

Chapter four: Creating Images That Excite Followers

Another thing that you will need to do for you Instagram is to know how to create pictures that people want to see and will keep them coming to you and not other people. Remember that Instagram can get crowded. Do not get lost, instead, stand out. This is easier than people think because you just need some good tips to make this happen for yourself. Most people are not professional photographers and they use their phones. However, today, you can make a phone picture a professional-looking picture, which is what we need here.

When you think of old photos you probably think of a full set up and honestly, this is a great way to take good photos and you can still use a full set up. The older times took great pictures and they were able to last throughout the ages. This shows that they did something right. However, in today's society, nearly everything is done digitally and this is because of the advances in technology that we have. For most people, it is just easier to use your phone. In this chapter, we will give you amazing tips on how to take great photos that will gain you followers and excite them.

A good tip for you to take into account is that you should take what is known as a customer-centric photo. When you are posting to your page, think about a few things before you hit the share button. Is your customer or follower going to benefit from the picture? Is it going to have some sort of value to what they want? Is this going to be a photo that is going to keep your followers interested or make them interested? You want to stay relevant to your followers and you always need to think about your brand or the products that you are selling in terms of the benefits for your customer or your followers. This is what is called focusing your marketing content for your benefit.

The first-rate images are those that will display your stocks, your brand or your niche and use it to show the people that are following you that you are staying relevant and engaging them. This keeps users interested and they will keep checking your profile to see which photos are being chosen and how they are being used. You can also get free advertising with helpful collaborations from followers who posted them. This would also keep users interested in checking your profile because they would like to see if their photo is the one that gets elected or to see if their friend is the one that you will choose. It is a really fun and creative way to keep your audience engaged and checking your profile every day. Everyone loves things like this because they are always talking to their friends seeing if you are going to choose their picture or if you are going to choose their friend's picture and who the lucky winner, things of that nature is.

Another great example is if you are a person whose niche is traveling, you are posting a picture of a waterfall or a bridge, and you are jumping in front of it or dancing in front of it. You want to be enthusiastic which is going to encourage your followers to get involved. They love to see beautiful pictures and this what you are creating for them here. They would probably share that picture and they would probably tag their friends in it as well or they may even get inspired to do some traveling themselves so that they can take a picture of their own that looks like yours.

Thanking people is also a really great idea to go with producing exciting and engaging content because it validates the people following you and it expresses great service and great care. A terrific example here is if you were doing a promotion and you got a lot of people that were commenting and sharing your picture, you could take the time and say thank you. It may take a little time to thank all the people that are doing this, but it is really going to make a difference in your page.

You can remember also that there is a rule of thirds. When applying this to your pictures, it is applied by aligning whatever subject you are trying to photograph with literal guidelines and inspection points before making the inspection points into squares and authorize the image to circulate from sector to sector.

This will design energy and interest. Luckily, our phones have an area that can do this for you. A great idea that you can use is if you are in front of a door, you can stand in the middle of it and distance your grid and this will offer an instant impact. Pay attention to all the details and make sure that you are varying your idea along these lines to design an alternative that engages your followers. You can also make a trademark style that is just your own and this is crucial for stick out and finding success when people visit your page.

You desire them to have an idea of what your work is like but no one else's and what kind of things they can expect from you. Instead of thinking about each individual photo, you can think ahead and plan out your feed. Another idea you can use a color palette or a color style. This will help as we mentioned before and a quick tip from experts that have mastered the craft is to choose a warm neutral color or cold color palette for your Instagram. Neutral is generally minimal and is best used for home brands, lifestyles, and fashion. Warm photos are generally great for travel bloggers while cold photos can best be seen in nature. So playing with the color pallets is a great idea for you to use.

Another tip that could really be helpful here is using employee Instagram photos. Personality and putting faces to names is essential because nobody chooses to interact with a corporation that is faceless. A great example of this is what JetBlue does. JetBlue is one of the biggest Twitter's on the scale and this is because they engage with their followers. They not only engage with the people, they always have really enthusiastic photos that are innovative and creative. This is to let you know that they are not just a faceless company.

They are a company that cares about the people that work for them and they want you to know that they care about you as well. Other people on Instagram have now followed JetBlue's example so that they could do the same thing and that they could reap the benefits as well. If you are focusing on employees, you can also focus on the personalities or birthdays. Even just an inventory count or a small personal touch adds so much life to a photo.

Another great idea for taking great photos that will excite your followers is to create a contest. Contests can be a significant engagement factor with Instagram. It is so effortless to gain followers through contests and having constant updates. Many people who do a contest will reward their fans with a hashtag or a prize, they do a collaboration with photos so that they can get recognized, and other people can get more followers as well. This can be a great way to get companies to see you as well so it's really a double benefit because you're not only getting yourself followers but you're also getting followers that can be of a higher pedigree and can help take you to the next level with branding and selling products if you're an influencer or a business owner.

They can also help you with your niche because they can introduce you to people who can find you, followers, which you might need for projects in the future. Another great thing about Instagram that is really great for finding followers is that you can use product photos. Product photos stand out very well because they can be simple or complicated but as long as it shows off all the available colors or the benefit of the item, you will be able to get followers in that same field. A great example of this is to look at the people on Instagram that love books. They have an entire genre on the app called bookstagram. Many people take a photo of the book that they have gotten in a book box or in a store and they add great props next to it. They could be anything from a necklace or if it is, a medieval book then they might have an ancient crown, rings, flowers, anything to make the photo stand out. The main focus, however, is the book, which would be the product. Many bookstagram photos actually get thousands of likes within the first day and this is a great thing to take advantage of.

Now a trick that is not as well known is a blogger Instagram photo. This is something that is going to keep your post interesting and you can have a regular feature such as a blogger on your page. Prominent bloggers have their individual fan base so they can actually bring their fans to you by working with you for your page and bloggers usually know how to make great photos because they already have their own website that needs them. You can take advantage of this for yourself and bring people to you quickly, which is another helpful tool.

If you are using a phone to take get Instagram pictures then the first thing that you are going to need to do to make your photo pop is to adjust your camera settings. You may think that you do not really need a lot of knowledge of the basic camera settings. Most people just use their smartphones, take pictures, and play with the filters that Instagram offers you but if you learn about the camera settings and how they work you will be able to take better pictures. Therefore, you should actually try to learn the settings.

Many photographers know that taking an underexposed photo is a great opportunity to take a good photo. When you are an amateur photographer and you are just starting out many people make the common mistake of taking a photo using full exposure or using full brightness. In the process of taking extremely bright pictures, the highlights and the details of the original picture are going to get lost. You need to learn how to adjust the exposure of your camera and shoot your pictures in lighting that is a little bit darker. You can also adjust the exposure on the brightness of the subject during the post-production editing that you will do before you post a picture to Instagram.

You also should not rely on autofocus either. If you are in the moment and taking that kind of photo then it is okay to use autofocus, but it is also better to learn how to control your focus manually instead of relying on it.

A beautiful picture can do a lot for your Instagram profile and for your Instagram page and a really simple way to learn how to do the manual focus feature is as follows. All you have to do is tap on the specifics of your subject that you want to highlight and then take the photo. You will get a well-focused and clean photo for Instagram. Turning off the HDR on your camera is another great idea because it can make your photos look overdone and over-processed. Over-processed and overdone pictures do not really do much to drive engagement on your Instagram account.

You should avoid using the flash as well. Flash is a useful tool but sometimes it can ruin the overall quality of the photo that you are taking. What the flash does is it blows out the lighting of the picture so it makes the picture look like it was captured with a camera that is disposable. This is not always the look that you are trying to achieve. If you are interested in enhancing the photo skills that you have a course in digital photography can actually really be beneficial. Otherwise, just have a basic understanding of the camera settings on your smartphone and try to avoid using flash too much.

You also should not overdo it with filters. Yes, Instagram has great filters and they make awesome filters for your images but you do not have to use filters just for the sake of using filters. If you do like using filters just make sure that, you are not getting carried away. If you are utilizing too strong a filter on your picture, you can ruin the natural lighting that your picture already has. So if you are using one do not overdo it by applying the filter to the fullest option that it has. Instead, stop the intensity the moment you start noticing that the picture is changing from the natural lighting. The best way to deal with filters is to keep experimenting with different levels to identify the level that you like to use in your pictures. You should also be mindful when you are selecting your filters to ensure that they are aligning with the overall theme of your Instagram feed or niche.

If you need another good idea, try turning your phone upside down. A lot of people suggest flipping your mobile phone upside down and taking pictures of your subject from the ground. It is believed by many that this is the best way of adding foreground elements. A photo taken from the ground is more interesting because the audience gets a better look at the object and it also gives more depth to the picture. Groundworks as a clever foreground element. Pictures like this can really boost your engagement rate on Instagram. Think about it like this. In the modeling world when they are trying to get a better picture of the model on a shoot, many times they will shoot the pictures from down below because it makes the model look longer and leaner. You can use that same application to your photos.

The composition is another area where you will receive help on your photos. To have a composition that is successful, you need to find a way to get your viewers to your photo and the picture should be capturing an emotion or story. When you are composing a photo, you should make sure you are aware of a few tricks.

We all know that when you take a photo you need good lighting because the lighting is one of the most important things that you can do for a photo. So when you are concentrating on lighting, be sure to keep the following things in mind. If you are using an iPhone, you can take really great photos when there is enough light. However, you can with others as well. If you are shooting indoors, then you should sit by your window and away from any light that is artificial because it could turn your photographs yellow and natural light will capture a picture much better anyhow. You also need to shoot at the right time if you are planning on taking photos. For instance, at dusk, it is going to result in really stunning light contrasts or soft shadows and there is nothing that is more essential for taking a good photo than the perfect light.

The same perks can be said for what is known as the golden hour. This is because the golden hour is where your subject is able to be backlit and it gives you a really beautiful result and saves time with editing because you can see everything that you need to without having to change it. Another great tip you can use is that instead of avoiding gray weather. You should embrace it. Cloudy days are genuinely great for shooting pictures because the light will spread out everywhere and this means that you can effectively do much more in the post-production when you are editing this photograph.

For specific types of photos that you are trying to do there are also unique tips that are specific to those photos. For example, if you are taking a food photo you need to find a photogenic spot like a wooden table or a slab of marble or anything else that can work as a simple backdrop but a textured backdrop for the food. If you can sit near the window so that you will get the natural light you can also increase the sharpness, contrast, and exposure and get a little fade out and it would make a great picture.

If you are a traveler and you want to take a great Instagram photo in nature, then you can go all out. You want a place that you want to see and make sure that you have a wide backdrop and that you are able to enter in a focal point. When you are editing your photos after being sure that, you are doing this properly as well. It is not just taking photos for Instagram, you need to edit it and make sure that it is the best that it can be before you put it out. This is what is going to engage your audience and make a difference. There are many different apps and that you can use to edit your pictures each having their own benefits and each having their own downfall. It is really interesting to play with them and see which one is going to work best for your photos and your Instagram.

A great tip for Instagram or any other social media account that you might have is that a little bit goes a long way and you do not have to be zealous. When they first became popular, the users began to go crazy because they had never been able to work with filters before and that is something that is tending to stay with people when it should not have. When you are finished editing your photos you need to take a step back, come back to the photo later and then check to see if you have overdone it. If you are using any filter, you should keep it simple and put the scale down to an intensity level of three to six.

With so many options that we have available to us, it's very fun to be able to go overboard or to use every photo editing tool that you have, but if you're a beginner stick to these three rules. Saturation, contrast, and brightness. Move between the edited and the original versions to make sure that you can find a fit that would work for your page and photographs. Remember to consider your viewpoint as well. Taking photos from a different vantage point will provide an all-new perspective. Even when it comes to a familiar subject. You can shoot from above or below as we have already talked about and you can go sideways or find an odd angle.

Just remember to be careful and do not break a limb trying to get the perfect shot. Do not hurt yourself just get inventive and creative. Leaving space around the focal point of your photo can add another visual interest instead of leaving it in you could have many details that will make the photo even better like the moon, the sky or the sun in the sky. Even a cloud that looks like something. If you want to focus on the focal point just have your photo subject into the draw in the line of your viewer and in photography, this is called a leading line. A leading line is a line that will draw the viewer to what you want them to see. This could be a road or a natural element like a tree.

Keep an eye out for a leading line and use them to add this to your photo. You can also add depth to your photo as well. It is what is going to give your photo something extra and it offers the photo and the viewer something to look at which will draw them in. Depth can uncover beautiful things in a photo. The best part about this, however, is that you can get creative when you are taking photos for Instagram. You can get very creative in how you want to do this and you do not have to get caught up in your feed or other issues. You can still be creative on your own because you want to stand out.

You should challenge yourself to do something different to add an extra pop as well. Symmetry is also pretty pleasing to the eye no matter where you see it so this is something to learn about. You can create interest by either using vertical symmetry or using the elements around you.

You can use patterns because our brains love patterns and some Instagram accounts have actually got a huge following by making or documenting beautiful patterns. Our brain loves wonderful visualizations like this. Vibrant colors is another really big trend right now because minimalism is trendy and neutrals are coming into play. A lot of times, you just crave that pop of color too. You can use bright colors or rich colors that will make you happy and give you energy. That will bring the viewers to you so that you can see better pictures and so that they can see they are offering them as your followers.

Humor is another great thing that you can use in your pictures. Instagram tries to be a happy place, which means that your humor will be able to be used for a good benefit. This is especially true in contrast to the other photos that you will see on this platform. Funny photos can offer a great breath of fresh air for your audience and show them that you understand what it is like to stop and smell the roses and be able to love what is going on in your life. It also shows that you do not have to take the world so seriously. The world is already a really serious place and everyone needs a splash of humor at some point. Offering your audience that is a great way to make sure that they stay engaged with you and your brightening up someone's day.

Another trick that you can use for your Instagram? Heads up because this tip is great but a little bit complicated is capturing a subject in motion. This is tough to do which is why it is so impressive if you can actually pull it off. An action shot is arresting but it is also exciting. It turns even an ordinary subject into something beautiful and lovely.

You do not always have to strive for perfection either. Sometimes a blurred moment can give it a dreamy but artistic touch from times in the past. When you are taking action photos to be sure to take multiple options so that you can increase your odds of having that great shot. You can use the burst mode by holding down the camera button on your phone to capture ten photos per second.

Sharp focus or an uninspected or interesting detail can also be great for grabbing your audience's attention. This is what has called a detail shot. You can offer a sense of stillness for calm or using the editing tools, you can create a photo that has enhanced detail.

Taking your photo from the closest viewpoint is also a great thing to preserve the quality of the shot. If you shoot from far away and crop this lowers the image resolution, which leads to a lackluster photo that could damage your brand. Another useful tip is to make sure that you are uploading photos that are sized to fit Instagram. We have already discussed food and how everybody loves a food shot and we have talked about people as well. When you are about to take a stunning portrait of a person you need to follow the natural light while you choose an appealing background and the tips that we used above. If you are able to utilize those to your benefit, you will be able to get a great shot of a person that will engage your audience and keep them wanting to see more selfies of you or more pictures of you. Even though we have mentioned the food shots before, we will say that one of the great things that you can do with food is to shoot from above because it offers a much more appealing angle for the food.

Animals are another thing that really sticks out to people. We love animals and everyone (usually even if they say they do not) likes them. There is at least one animal that people do like. So since everybody loves animals your shots on Instagram photos have been shown to be better if there is a cute animal in them and it opens you up to all the people that love animals and have a following that loves animals as well. Not only will you bring them to you but also you are bringing their fans to you.

Another simple trick that you can use is a captivating background. You can take advantage of an awesome background and make your photo a thousand times better. It is the reason that you want to take a selfie in a restaurant that has amazing wallpaper or the reason that you want to take a photo in front of a wall that has graffiti or things of that nature. It is because you saw something in the background that you liked and you wanted to capture that shot so that people could see it as well. The more creative your background the better you can use the shot. Flowers or anything that is really going to make your photo stand up would work, but this could take your photo to the next level because people will be loving what they see and this is why so many people take pictures in front of walls or other places. It is because they realize that that background is something that people are going to want to see.

If you follow the tips and tricks in this chapter, you should be able to provide your audience with captivating photos that are going to keep followers coming to you and that is going to make them want to stay with your page. We have also given you some great tips on how to play with your camera so that you can have the tools at your disposal to keep learning and improving your photos as well. This is a good thing to remember because Instagram is all about growth.

Chapter five: How To Be Influential

When you create an Instagram account, another thing that you will need to be able to understand is how to be influential and to be authoritative. Authoritative means that you are self-confident and you are a person to be obeyed and respected more. Alternatively, it also means that you are someone who is reliable and telling the truth. Influential means that you have a great influence on something, which means that you have an effect on people's behavior or effect.

To be influential on Instagram you will need to learn how to set up your account and your bio to make sure that you can get as many people to follow you as you possibly can. So one of the things that you will need to do is make sure that you are utilizing your bio properly instead of incorrectly. Since Instagram only gives you one clickable link, you need to make sure that you are using it right. You can be enticed to send Instagram users straight to your website's homepage but if you do you will be missing out on the opportunity to collect information on Instagram and design long-lasting relationships while you do so. There are many things that you can do as if a landing page with an offer for your Instagram followers and building one can be very beneficial. You can offer anything from an eBook or having your followers subscribing to your newsletter or you could even give you a special discount for 25% off an item or 10% off if you would like to offer less.

This will also be able to give you the opportunity to use extra attention from Instagram to drive conversions to you. You should also make sure that you are checking out your highlights and that you are spicing up your Instagram stories. This will let you save the best parts from your stories and it will let you offer new content to the people who follow you. Create a channel on your homepage and remember that you need a consistent and solid strategy. A solid and consistent strategy is going to help you as well. The primary rules for content creation are to have a theme for your account or an aesthetic or niche. Using videos will generate engagement and bring followers to you as well and you should be consistent. You need to have a consistent message and remember that you should be posting as often as you can so that your followers are loyal and they can see that you are taking this seriously.

Another thing you need to be able to ability to post as often as possible. Remember that the more you post the quicker you grow. Instagram is a visual platform. Posting attractive content is key. To be noticed you should try to put out the best pictures that you can.

Videos are a great idea to use for your accounts as well and you may be surprised to learn that videos make up over fifty percent of mobile traffic as early as three years ago. Imagine how much mobile traffic it would make up now. Along with this, you can get into your Instagram stories. These are so popular and they disappear after a single day (a solid twenty-four hours). You may not think that this is a good idea for marketing but it can be. Stories sit at the very top of someone who is feed. Therefore, even though your posts may not be getting a lot of followers, your stories might gain the attention you need. Another reason that this could work is that business users incorporate links in their stories, which is an additional bonus. Although there is another reason that the stories are so good as well. They give you a chance to enjoy the ability to take a few risks or experiment with content that is a bit different.

You should also consider doing things that do not scale which means that you need to do things that cannot be programmed. Do things that you can do. Add a personal touch to your profile and it will reflect in the results that you want to see. Some great tips that you should follow up on are that you should do your best to reply to the comments whilst your account is small and it will pay off to help it get larger. Use your name in your comments as well to let the people know that they are talking to you and not a bot. Explore different hashtags to see what it is that people are discussing and even take advantage of being able to join a conversation on a competitor page.

Growing influence on Instagram means that you have the opportunity for a great outreach and a great opportunity to gain influence with other influencers or businesses. Personal relationships with Instagram mean that you are sending emails, and contacting everyone directly. You may even have to meet people face to face.

Instagram has a full range of features and you should take advantage of them. If you want to have people see a wide range of your content and you have the option to use many different features. You can use highlights, carousel posts, and stories to benefit your profile and drive people to you.

Take advantage of contests. We have mentioned this a little above, but it is worth mentioning again because contests can drive hundreds of people to your page. The simplest option that you can use for your profile is to offer prizes to the users on Instagram that will share the contest and invite all of their friends to join in as well. This will bring new followers to your page and it does not have to cost a whole lot for you to do.

You should also invest some time trying to endorse your Instagram to optimize who can see your content and gain new people. Spend time promoting your page on your other pages and places online if you like and you will bring more people to you. You just need to make sure that you keep your public accounts and personal accounts separate. This will eliminate the danger. You need to get your brand out there and a great way to do it is promotion. A tip that most people do not utilize is that if you are asked to do an interview you should do it even if it is just for a small article. You should always say yes even if it is a small publication. Small publications have a more committed following and as such; you can use that to your advantage. Remember to mention your Instagram account.

Benefit from what a shout out can do for you. When you want to grow your brand, you need to build a partnership. This is very true on social media and a post from someone important could influence thousands of new people that use the site. Therefore, you should take advantage of this and make sure that you are making good connections. If you can try to work with other influencers. The great thing about influencers is that they can shout out to you and gain you additional followers and spread your brand further. If you approach them directly, more than likely you will have to pay for a shootout but be smart and ready to negotiate. There are also agencies that can serve as a go-between and can help you with this to make it easier. They also pair willing influencers and paying brands based on relevance.

Another thing that many people do is what is known as sharing back. This is when someone shares something of yours so you share something of theirs in return. This ultimately gets you more shares. The reason is that other people want more shares too so when they see that your willing to share their posts they will be willing to share yours.

A good idea to follow is that you should not follow an account that will have thousands of followers if you do not because it has not considered fair. You should work with users that have the identical amount of followers that you do and make sure that your both getting a fair deal out of it because that will benefit both of you in a fairway. If there is a discrepancy, you can share for a share with someone who has a slight amount of more followers than you do but not too much.

Everyone loves free stuff and you can capitalize on this in a big way. Provide your followers or potential followers with something new and of value. Pair it with influencer marketing and you have something you could really use to gain yourself a great following. The best part? Free stuff can be anything. You could offer a prize or a service to people that they need and bam! Instant followers.

Embracing analytics is a great tool for yourself as well. It is easy to do this when you understand the different aspects of the data. The main parts of the data that you should be aware of are how to understand how to track your growth and see what influencers are already following you and you can see how to choose the right partners. Make sure you know your content rates and engagement rates as well.

One of the most important tips we have for you, however, is on what not to do. These can be just as important. Instagram keeps a much-updated list of hashtags that have been banned. Therefore, when you use one of these in your posts, that post will not appear in the searches. When you do this repeatedly, you are running the risk of getting shadowbanned. Avoid going overboard with your hashtags as well. Use the ones that are the most relevant.

Shadow bans exist to make sure that the users are deterred from using a specific kind of behavior that is not appropriate, is abusive, or considered to be spam. In the case of Instagram, the platform seems to essentially be targeting users who displayed unsuitable behavior or they are displaying inappropriate pictures or content. What is interesting is that the non-spam behaviors have also been lumped in and you can get shadowbanned with this kind of behavior now as well. The biggest example of this is using the same hashtags repeatedly. In fact as early as a few months ago this year, Instagram posted a statement that explained that they understand that users are having to experience different issues with hashtags because they keep using them over and over and it explained that they are trying to improve this system, but they also told their users that they recommend on focusing on a goal rather than a hashtag.

They were saying that having a growth strategy is more essential to success on Instagram and hashtagging while giving tips to their users on how to become better storytellers. It's the only time that Instagram has ever actually confirmed that there's an issue with hashtag searches but however, they didn't admit to implementing a shadowban on the users instead they just said that they were improving their system. Some tips to make sure that you do not get a shadowban placed on you are that you should not use hashtags that are banned or hashtags that can be invaded with inappropriate content. Now this one is hard because a very innocent hashtag can become involved with inappropriate content, that is not your fault, and most people are not even aware of it so they get in trouble when they have not really done anything wrong.

Do not use algorithms, bots or automation that violate Instagram's terms of use. In a later chapter of this book, we explain how automation is completely illegal and you should not be using them anyway but we also go into the details of why people think they are useful as well. This book, however, does not recommend that you use them. We recommend staying away from them completely. You should also avoid big surges in your Instagram activity. Instagram has limits in place on how many photos you can like, comments you can leave and even how many accounts you can follow or unfollow, but everyone's limits are different, and it is based upon different factors. The reason that Instagram is imposing these limits on user activity is to crack down on bots because they are illegal. If all of a sudden you are following fifty or more accounts and you immediately unfollow half of them Instagram interprets this, as a bit of automation activity and your account will get shadowbanned as a result.

You should also try to avoid being reported by other users as well. A big way to show up on Instagram's shadowban radar is to be reported by another user for doing something wrong. It is important to know, however, that getting reported alone is not enough for them to take action against your account. You would have to actually violate their terms of service and they would have to determine that you actually did this. However, if they do determine that you are at fault they are not just going to shadow ban you. They could and in most cases will fully disable ban your account if it is serious enough. There are ways to tell that you are on Instagram's shadowban list and one way is to use someone else's account and see if your posts appear in hashtag searches. If they do not, then it is more than likely that you have been shadowbanned. If you ask a friend to unfollow your account and then search for one of the hashtags you use in a recent post. If your post does not appear under the hashtag then you have been shadowbanned. There is even a shadowban analyzer tool that people have been recommending to see if your accounts have been shadowbanned. However, this tool is not entirely accurate and it is not recommended that you use it. You should not fall into the game of people trying to get you to use it.

To get yourself off the shadowban list you should stop using broken hashtags or banned hashtags and you should stop using auto posting software and bots. Other users have said that taking a couple of days off Instagram has actually helped lift the shadowban. If you decide to take a break just avoid doing anything on the app for at least two days. You can also report your shadowban to Instagram and see if they will review your case again or tell you what you have done wrong. They may let you fix it. You should be aware though however, social media platforms are extremely difficult to get a hold of and while they do have a support email that does not guarantee that they are going to email you within a specific amount of time.

Another thing that you really need to understand about becoming influential on Instagram is that you need to know your trade. You have to know what it is that you are intending to do and what you are intending to talk about. Remember that we have said this before, you have to know what your niche is and you have to have knowledge in that niche. The last thing you want is for somebody to ask you a question and you were not able to answer because you do not have the knowledge that you need to have. It is more than just posting selfies to your page. It is important to understand that you are selling point has information and that your customers are going to need to see that. Once you are able to give them that information this is how you get more people to want to come to you because they realize that you are an expert on what you are talking about and if you are not an expert in that, you are at least knowledgeable with what you are talking about.

You should also create content that people want to see. We said this before as well, but remember that you need to get those likes, and you need to get those shares. Great photography is something that is appreciated on Instagram and other social media platforms and with Instagram's filters and editing tools, this has become a lot easier. Just make sure that you can have great pictures without doing too much. Remember the tips that we have shared about not going overboard with those filters and it will really help you.

User-generated content is what is known as content that has to do with your niche, which is what we have already discussed. However, this differs a little bit because it helps put people into the spotlight. When you are able to give people the spotlight, they are going to go and get excited about your friends and share with their friends as well. Cross-promotion is also a great way to get some exposure. Instagram allows you to share your photos to other platforms like Twitter or Facebook and it also lets you embed your Instagram photos in your blog posts so you can cross-promote yourself or have your followers do it for you and then you'll be able to get more followers and become more influential that way as well.

This is a trick that many people use for marketing but you can use it for your Instagram as well. In social media, everything keeps evolving. It also keeps growing and trends come and go on the regular. It is very important to keep up with trends and stay ahead of them. For instance the hashtag. A hashtag is a trend but it is still prevalent and it has not gone away. It has been gaining traction and it is obvious that this is a trend that is not going to go away for a while.

Sponsored posts are more likely to be noticed by a larger number of Instagram users and keeping up with the changes to new trends is definitely going to help you develop your own presence on social networks. Reaching out to people is also something that we mentioned but people do not realize just how beneficial this could be. A great example would be if you are interested in fashion and you saw a woman in a beautiful dress. For this, we are going to say it looks like it was handmade. You could say something in the comments like, 'This is amazing! Did you make that?' or 'Oh my gosh! This looks so one of a kind! Where were you able to find it?' By doing this, you will be encouraging them to answer you and by reaching out to them, you have just developed a connection.

If you cannot find a hashtag that supports your niche, make your own. If you have a product, that you are marketing or something that you are trying to develop for your brand make a hashtag yourself! People can click on the account name and they will be able to see your hashtags instantly. They will know exactly what it is and it really helps you grow your presence. Another way to reach out to people is if you have a poster or an image that you think a specific brand name or an influencer would like. Use that to your advantage and tag them in it. It is so easy to tag people's names so that they can see your posts. To avoid annoying people, you should do this sparingly and you should not do this every time you post something that has to do with that person. You can tag magazines and other influencers, even celebrities!

A great example is book authors. Many book authors' especially young adult book authors are on Instagram and they are constantly sharing pictures of their books. They also constantly offer giveaways. In particular, when you win something from them, you can thank them for what they have sent you and then you can tag their name in it. By doing so, more often than not, they will respond to you in a very friendly way and you just developed a connection with someone who has a massive following.

Sometimes just because something looks pretty it does not mean you should always post it. It is important to stay on your niche or your brand. If you want to post it, post it to your personal account instead of your brand account. You always have to be careful to stay on a brand because a lot of people will only work with the people that are on their brand. This next tip may not seem like a very effective way to be more influential online, but sometimes you just have to get involved in the offline community as well. This includes going to meetups or events organized around Instagram. For this kind of thing, you have to remember to be safe and if something feels wrong then do not do it. The reason that we stress this is because meetups are supposed to be safe and they're supposed to be made so that you can meet other people in the same field that you're in, but in today's society it's always better to be safe than sorry.

Be sure that you are publishing plenty of content that is free as well. The more valuable content you publish the more you are going to establish your brand as an authority in the field that you have chosen for yourself. In the area of marketing where people are being bombarded with content, they like value so you can give them something that they can really get involved in or something that they really like such as a free eBook. You will not only establish your brand and credibility but you will also add them to your email list and then get them to buy your products.

The more quality you create the better. It is been said by recent studies that over half of marketers create at least one piece of new content each week. You also need to make sure that it is simple to access. No one is a fan of sites that require you to give them the email address, phone number, income, how many homes you have had in the past five years and all the extra information that is unnecessary. You can require an email address so that you can have people in your database but even that is not a necessary factor. In today's society, if you are really trying to drive value with what you are offering, they will come back for more so you do not need all the extra attention and steps. That is just going to bother your customers and your followers.

When you are on social media platforms, you have the option of links. You have the knowledge and people need it. When you can help them, they will come to you but bring their friends to you as well. You can also do what is known as a guest post. Freelance writers will be familiar with this one. Guest posting or guest blogging is a really useful tool when you are just starting out. Freelance writers, in particular, understand this one because when they are trying to get more writing jobs and a better chance of people recognizing who they are, they will do a lot of guest posts to get some great files for their profile and it helps get their name out there. Like anything in this world, this can be used incorrectly.

Your goal with blogging on somebody's post or guest posting is to find popular but well-liked blogs that will be able to talk at the audience that you are trying to reach for yourself. You need to find your unique voice as a guest poster but remember that you need to deliver what others can't and what will make you stand out. This is a really good chance for you to shine in your area of expertise as well as reach people that you might not have been able to connect with on your own. You can be picky about the channels that you want to post ideas to or post on or you can spread yourself a little thinner and say yes to as many as you choose.

If the thought of speaking to a room full of customers does not give you stage fright then you can give public speaking a good try as well. This also helps to get your name out there and it gets your products in your brand out there. You just need to stay true to your core message and know what you want to be known for. Now that we have talked about how you can be influential, we will now talk about how to be authoritative. We have explained the difference above, so we will not do so again. We are going to be explaining a few different tricks and tips that you can use here as well and it will let you have the opportunity to be a driving force on your page. Another way to grab people's attention is to intrigue them or entertain them. Entertainment leads to great opportunities and the reason that it is effective is that people naturally enjoy being entertained. We are drawn to fun things and it is just how our brains are wired. We also love to be intrigued and we love the opportunity to explore new things and to learn new things. You can also approach the topic from a different angle. One of the biggest challenges in content marketing or social media platforms is that most topics have already been written about and they have been written about extensively. One way to get attention from a topic that has already been talked about so much is to approach it from a different angle and give people a new idea.

Reply to authorities. The simple act of associating with other authorities will raise you up and makes you more authoritative as well. Along with this, you should also quote the authorities and this is something that everyone loves. Authorities love engagement too so if you reply to authorities and quote authorities this could help. This could be something as simple as a shout out or something that they said, but you could turn it into a blog post and then mention what they have said. After this, you can share it with them and give them credit for sparking the idea that you have had. Compliment them and make sure that you are giving them the credit that is owed to them. This is very important because if you do not give them the credit that they deserve, you can get in trouble.

You could also co-create with other authorities on Instagram or build offline recognition, which is something we talked about with being influential as well. You can do something that is unique too. Anyone can post on Facebook or Instagram and people do this all the time. You are probably not going to be an expert right away but you still should avoid doing the same thing that everybody else does. As such, you need to do something that is different from what they are doing or bigger than what they are doing so that they can set you apart.

Basically what you're trying to do with Instagram is that you're trying to think about the long-term and you're trying to make sure that you can keep building your followers, not just now but over time as well. Try writing from the mindset of a real expert and this should demonstrate your authority as well. Rather than writing a simple guide to what restaurant is the best you could step up and make it a complete guide with great pictures and examples.

You can also site real illustrations and facts. It is simple to hypothesize about concepts but it is hard to validate them. This is why it is needed as an authority to cite examples and categorically stay as truthful and honest as possible. This is very important because remember an authoritative person is an honest person. You can also link to outside sources if you using information that comes from different people and if you are making statements about people that have already had ideas that you are trying to bring attention to, make sure that you are giving them credit. You should be available for inquiries if someone is trying to talk to you as well. If someone wants information about something that you posted or something that you have written, make sure that you are available to answer their questions. One of the hardest things about being influential and authoritative is that you will have to let go of the reins and let people actually read what you have done or see your pictures. It can be really scary to open yourself up to people but Instagram is all about sharing content and posting content so you are going to have to put yourself out there, but if this is hard for you then it might be a little bit difficult to do this at first because it can be daunting. Just know that you can do it and while it takes a little time to get used to it, it will get easier over time.

You should also learn how to self-edit. You need to get to the point where you can read over your own writing and determine whether it makes sense. This is going to make your posts a lot easier to understand, a lot easier to read and one of the most important things that you can do to have an authoritative presence. Communication is important and there are many different ways to do this. Everyone usually has their own way of doing this but whatever the case of collaboration that you are doing and whatever type of communication that you are trying to do, make sure that people can understand it and make sure that it is clear. You're not going to be an expert in everything that you write about or that you post about right away, but the trick is to figure out a way to make it sound like you are and another thing that you need to do is make sure that your writing is clean so that people can read it and they're not scratching their heads trying to figure out what it is you're trying to say. The tips and tricks in this chapter are designed to help you become a driving force on Instagram and make sure that people remember who you are. If you follow these tips and tricks, you should have a much better presence on Instagram and you will be able to get people to follow you.

Chapter six: How To Create Interesting Content

Our next section is going to be all about how you can produce quality content that is interesting and engaging. This is going to be able to take your Instagram to a higher level and the best part about this is that it is going to be able to gain you a better following and more people will want to see your content as it improves and has great quality that you can use for your benefit. People will want to see your page for the substance you provide and the best way to turn Instagram into a viable financial option for you is to produce the best content that you can.

Using templates can help you create great content and it helps so much when you are trying to produce better content. There are a lot of websites that offer some great templates and you will be able to change them to suit your needs as they come. If you use these, you do not even have to exert much effort and it can look incredible.

If you desire to establish a post that is, going to endorse a special offer this is also a great idea because maybe you need a template to announce a new opening time or maybe you want to push a recipe that you have been able to share on a blog. Whatever message you need to send, you can do it with the template and there are some great places that you can find them for free. You can edit copy and select them and you can do different colors and styles as well. It is a great way to make some real quality content on your Instagram. You can also find high-quality stock images as well for help. Stock images have a bit of a bad rap in new times but that has not to say that you should avoid utilizing them. They can actually aid make a diverse feed that will use other images and other templates. However not all stock images have what it takes to be a prime spot in your feed. Some are honestly pretty terrible and you need to make sure that their royalty-free.

You need high-quality photos that actually do not look stocky. There are a couple of different places that you can go and they offer a wide range of images for free. Because of this, you are bound to find something suitable, whatever you are niche. Once again, just make sure that the images are royalty-free; otherwise, you could be suffering from copyright infringement. Now on this same idea, if you want to make stock images that are unique you can also customize them by using overlays, filters, and icons on borders. Whatever it is that you like to do is what works and will be good for you.

You can repost Instagram content from brands within your niche as well. If you do not have time to make generate your personal content the good news is you may not have to. It might be the incident that other Instagram accounts are already doing a great job of producing amazing content that your audience is actually interested in and if you get permission from the brands to do so, you can repost them. When you can repost the content that is similar to yours or from an account that is relevant to your audience, just make sure that you get their permission first. You always have to reach out to the user for permission to repost because remember, it is their content that you are wanting to repost. As such, you cannot simply steal it, you need to make sure that you are approaching this through the proper way and making sure that you obtain their permission before you do anything with their content.

Once you reposted if you have permission to do so, you will need to give them the proper credit. Tag them and make sure that you are following the proper channels to do this correctly. Sharing videos and stories to your feed is another great way of creating content as well. Everyone loves to see the stories and everyone loves to see the videos, because that makes them feel like they are closer to you and that they have a real connection with you. It is also a great thing to do because people love seeing the video and our brains usually want to see this first in many cases. Pictures are great but you can be really drawn into a video in a way that a picture might not be able to do for you. However, on the flip side to this, you can be really drawn into a photo whereas you might not be drawn into a video.

Another great idea for good content is to use user-generated content. We talked about this a little bit before but the term applies to any content created by a user or any product or service that is about that product or service that the user is trying to create. Unless you are a giant or prominent brand, its likely users will create Instagram content about you and your products without an incentive. Get around this by running a competition where users could actually win something by creating an Instagram post about you.

Offering a follower a free product or a discount, for instance, will really gain traction. If you are running, a campaign where users can win something you will notice that they are creating posts and following your hashtags so that they can see what is going on with the contest. You can also publish your competition across your other social media channels or even include in a newsletter if you wanted to and you can monitor the performance of your campaign hashtag to see how well the contest is going as well and you can do this simply by using tools that Instagram offers free. You should not be too exclusive with the kind of content you request your users to post. Otherwise, the users are not going to bother. User-generated content should have an augmented method to source and content for your feed instead of being the focus. This is important because if you rely too much on user-generated content, your followers may feel like you are exploiting them and you will have less control over the aesthetic of your feed.

Collaborations with influencers is another great way to get your content to be the best that it can be. If you want more control over your feed and you need a consistent flow of on-brand Instagram content, you should seriously consider trying to work with influencers. If you collaborate with influencers that already have a good-sized following this lets them come to you. You have a great opportunity here to expand your following.

You would also have some great feed content that you can use to your advantage. If you are a small business with a small business budget or a small brand with a small brand budget then obviously you will want to connect with a micro-influencer rather than a big-name influencer. Micro-influencers usually have a following of people between ten thousand or even up to fifty thousand and it is very easy to strike a deal with them. However, the important thing to remember is that this is true only if you are what is known as an Instagram seller.

This means only if you are selling a product on Instagram or if your brand is selling something on Instagram that their audience is going to be genuinely interested in. If they know that their audience is not going to be interested in what your niche is, then they are not going to go with you. This is why you need to find an influencer that fits your niche and fits it well. So for example, if your niche is fitness, you may not be able to work with someone whose niche is traveling. This is because fitness and traveling do not necessarily go together. They can be brought together but it is not something that you typically see.

If you are a small brand, you are working with fitness, and you see a micro-influencer that has a following because they are posting workout routines, you are more likely to be able to work with them because you are both into fitness and your niches are similar. You can send a DM, which is like a private message on Instagram, and usually, influencers will have their contact information in their bio as well if you need them. Send them a private message and see if they would be willing to work with you and more often than not they're very kind and they're actually more likely to work with you so that they're able to experience some benefits as well and not just give you benefit.

One of the biggest reasons that you should be using Instagram for business and branding is to check out the facts. If you consider Instagram compared to other social media platforms like Twitter and Facebook, Instagram is able to get you fifty times more engagement than you have with Facebook. That is not a number to take lightly and it is something to really think about. If you have fifty times more engagement with followers on Instagram than Facebook use it. Use Instagram to your advantage and get those followers. It will also give you over a hundred times more engagement per follower than a Twitter account. Those numbers are huge! That is a big difference. This is why all of the big businesses and brands are jumping on Instagram and not the other social media platforms anymore. However, it is important to note that they still use them together with Instagram because they realized that there is a benefit to doing all of them together and you can amass a larger following.

It is also said that visual content is easier because it is quick and it does not take as much time as written content. Another benefit that it offers is that you can look at it without much effort at all. This is why Instagram is a hot commodity and it is a hot favorite for users around the web to use. It just takes time to get this right. When you first get on Instagram you might think that this is going to be the easiest thing you've ever done and all you have to do is snap a picture but it's more than that. You need to create the right pictures along with the need to get engagement. You also have to have ideas and reach your audience. All of these things could be a very challenging task. However, once you start doing it understanding Instagram and what you need for it will get easier and you begin to take better pictures and understand the content better as well. Just keep reminding yourself that it does get easier because you are getting used to it.

Many people ask the question of why high-quality content is so important and it is because you have to rethink your content strategy and your photos if you want to stay relevant because everybody is using Instagram now. Instagram is not meant to stop you from growing your business it's meant to help you grow it but it definitely will compel you to rework your Instagram content strategy so that you can create the best content for Instagram and make sure that the people are still interested in what you have to say and what you have to show. You can plan your Instagram content strategy simply by asking who your audience is and what type of content you think they will want to see. Finding your audience and their likes and dislikes are going to take some time and we have mentioned in other chapters how you can get them to want to see your page and want to see what you have to say. All you have to do is keep rolling out that content and make sure that it is the best that you can give. If you are a jewelry brand for example then you should put out photos revolving around jewelry, but you should not just take a picture of a necklace on a display. Instead, what you should do is you should make sure that it looks beautiful and that it has great lighting so that your audience will be able to see it better. Make sure that they will be able to see the embellishments on the jewelry better and that it will be a picture that entices them to your page for maximum results. You can share all different content on Instagram and if you are sharing things that revolve around your niche, you should share what your brand is and what you believe. This little backstory type of set up really lets you connect with your audience and help them to gain trust and loyalty to you. Do not be a faceless corporation. Show them what you are about and what it is that you believe in and stand for.

Post what goes on in the workplace or your brand as well? These photos let the audience connect with you behind the scenes and not just the services that you provide. This can be a really fun and innovative way to get people to step up and notice you as well as wanting to follow you and see what you are going to do next. If you are a company, you can also allow your employees to share their perspective on behalf of the brand or product and you can share photos of people using the products that you sell for your brand or your business. A good tip for you to use is to remember to have fun being creative with your products as well and make sure that they are being photographed to the best of their ability.

You can command attention with a big idea and a big theme as well. At the end of the day, this is what people want to see and using a common theme that binds those images together is going to be the best for your profile and your page. If you are finding that you are having trouble being consistent with your postings there are ways to help with this as well. We have stressed the importance of being able to post as consistently as possible but if you're finding that this is hard for you send your audience posts at a specific time every day and this will make it easier. Having a routine in place and a schedule is a great idea for anybody on social media or even just in your regular life. This is because a schedule can keep things simple and easier for you. For example, if you want to post in the morning, make sure that you have set up to do so and then the rest of the day you do not have to worry about anything because you have already done it.

You should also consider Instagram as a source of micro-blogging. If you are able to move in the world of quick fixes and ready-made content, Instagram is picking this up because this is a trend called micro-blogging or you can use this for your product story in less than two thousand characters. This is a condensed form of blogging and it is a great way to display your products along with visual elements that will make your page stand out to the user. You can also share a tutorial, which is a great way to help solve people's problems; you could add an important update or even just telling them what is going on with your life for an update. Keep it short, concise and always make sure that it has a call of action. This is both engaging and enticing to your users.

Instagram is a platform where consistency is key, which is why we spent some time trying to explain why you should be posting as consistently as possible. However, if you are able to display your best work on your Instagram account it can also be an awesome portfolio of your skills and this has the ability, in turn, to be able to open you up to other opportunities for working with brands, collaborating on other social media accounts and being paid for your Instagram content. This is why many people are trying to use Instagram to gain better benefits. There are so many benefits to using Instagram these days and if you are able to use it to your benefit, you will be able to begin to get paid. This is what you want and what you are trying to achieve for yourself.

When you are shooting your photos, we have given you great tips in other chapters of this book on how to use your camera to the best benefit and that you do not need a fancy camera with all the accessories. Examples of what eel mean are things like lightboxes, tripods, and lenses. Now if you want to go professional like that, that is great but it is just not in everybody's budget. These things can add up really quickly and many people have other things that they have to pay for and that take precedence. If this is you and you just have your phone, do not fear. There are some great Instagram accounts that are all shot with a camera on their phone and the reason why they are successful is not that they are using the most expensive camera at all. The reason that their success is because the content and composition of the photos that the person is taking are good.

Start thinking about the angles of the photos that you can take and this will help your photos get to the next level as well. One tip, in particular, is to take as many photos as possible. Do not just take one or two. Think about taking ten or 15. Think about changing the composition, the distance that you are from the camera, the angle that you are taking your photos from and things of that nature. All of these things are going to make such a difference in the photo and not only will this mean that you will be able to pick the best photos to put on Instagram, but you will have more content in the future if you want to use the other photos that you are not using for this particular post.

A great example to make this easier for you to understand is to imagine that you are a food blogger. As a food blogger, you might want to post a photo of an amazing recipe that you created this week but then in a few more weeks' time, you might want to remind your followers of that recipe or you might want to send it into somewhere else. This is a great option for many users. By having a variety of different photos from the same shoot this means that, you can do that without repeating your content because the pictures will be different.

To make sure that you are creating engaging photos for your audience you also remember the need to edit using Instagram's editing tools and to take the time to study them and understand their benefit. Another great timesaving tip is for editing as well. This tip is to edit the content for the week in a single sitting. It may take longer to do it all at once but having all of your weeks' photos ready at the touch of a button is going to be so much easier than doing it individually one at a time. It also frees up extra time for you during the week so that you can focus on other parts of your Instagram as well. This is going to be a helpful tip because you need some extra time to think about what you are doing and to make sure that you are producing quality content. Therefore, by making sure that you are saving time for yourself, this gives you a chance to recheck everything and make sure that it is how you want it before you send it out.

Be strategic. When you are able to be strategic about your postings, this will help you have better content. If you wish to establish your Instagram account make sure that you've created a beautiful aesthetic and when you plan out your content avoid posting photos that are almost identical or have general similarities when placed side by side to each other. This is true even if they are just too close to each other. If they are too close together, your followers might get jaded of seeing the same content repeatedly. One of the easiest ways to plan your post is to make a schedule or write down how your plans to post your photos. If you've noticed on the schedule or on the piece of paper that you're planning out your photos on, that you have a set of dumbbells one week and then a set of them next week, you might realize that they are to close together on your page and that you may want to space them apart.

Do not forget also that you need to engage with your audience. Since they are taking the time to like and share your photos, you need to take the time to thank them for it and to be nice and complimentary to them so that they want to keep coming back to you. Another great way to engage your audience is to share an experience. Every day millions of people are scrolling through Instagram feeds and spending hours of their time doing so. As such, you should share a magical experience with them so that they want to come to you instead of other profiles. A great example of this is GoPro. Everyone has heard of GoPros and their cameras are so sought after that it is ridiculous. There were even people who have gotten hurt trying to obtain one which is insane because you should never hurt yourself trying to get a camera or anything else. The people who use GoPros however, are able to capture something more than just a picture. They are not just posting pictures of the cameras they are sharing the adventures that their cameras can capture. They are showing you a content post but they are also showing you experiences. One tip that many people have about GoPro cameras however, is that you need to be careful not to get hurt. This is because with a GoPro camera it is actually very easy to get hurt. So be very careful if you are going to choose to use them. There are so many others that are the same way. The GoPro account shows you beautiful pictures that are likely to catch your eye but they are also showing you an experience that the person behind the camera is going through and they are sharing it with you so that you can see it too.

Appealing to emotion is a great idea as well. Premium content engages users in different ways. For example, a shoe company that is famous has always focused on the idea that you should pay it forward. This is a concept that is very big right now as it should be. Everyone is seeming to realize that the world is not perfect and that there are many people around the world that really need help and they cannot get help. As such, a lot of brands and companies are realizing that they can take steps to help and this particular shoe company is doing its best to do that. For every shoe that you buy, they donate a pair to a child in a developing nation that is in need of help. To get other people to see this they show this idea through their Instagram with images that will appeal to your emotions and your heart not just your eyes. This is a very smart technique because it not only entices and engages people to follow them but it also opens their eyes to the problems of the world and how we can fix it.

Crowdsourcing can help here as well. If you are getting overwhelmed, they can help. Take a giant company that has recently crowdsourced its content. They used a life campaign and encouraged the users that followed them to tag useful tricks and hints related to a hashtag. As a result? They were bombarded with new content to post that was innovative, creative, fresh and new. It also enabled them to engage with their audience in a completely new way. In addition to those benefits, it established them as a brand of usefulness and more people came to them as a result. Coming up with a clever hashtag is a great way to inspire people to post for you and it can be fruitful for content.

Challenge your audience will capture the attention of your audience and increase your engagement for content. Try and post exciting images. The challenge does not have to be complicated or overly done. It just needs to keep their attention on you and your page. You could set deadlines and this will encourage the users to take action immediately and engage their friends as well. As you can see the size of the contests increases, you must remember that the prize should as well. A good example of what we mean is to think of a handmade company trying to get their name out there. Therefore, they make a set of contests and the first is small. As such, the prize might be small like a handmade hat or a beauty product. Then the next contest comes and it is bigger so they give away a blanket or a bigger ticket item. The last contest would be the biggest so they could give away a spa set along with coupons and vouchers for more products as well as a basket of free items or trial items. This would be a great way for your company to get their name noticed and the same is true for a brand.

For your pictures, we have already talked about the importance of having a focal point, but you should be aware of other photo tricks as well. One trick, in particular, is that you should also allow for borders and white space. Leaving white edges around the image can create a very unusual effect that will attract the eye more than an image with no border. This is going to be especially true if your image that you taking a shot of respects previous points such as the rule of thirds those we talked about and the focal point that we talked about as well.

Borders can also help ensure that the elements of the picture have room to breathe and the elements in the design have room to breathe. This is a very important aspect to consider if you want to avoid an overly busy post. Remember busy posts can cause your audience to turn from you instead of towards you. Another thing that you should also pay attention to that we have talked about a little bit is that contrast and the balance for an image can really cause it to stand out on an Instagram feed.

You should use contrasting elements for your images as well. This refers to many different aspects and some of the most basic ones are the following examples. Fonts, lights, exposure, and things of that nature. It is a great idea to play around with these because they give you valuable experience that you can use later to your benefit and the benefit of your page. You can play around with the filters that we have talked about and they should bring your picture to life as well. There are many different options that you can use for yourself and it should make a convincing post for people to tune into for your page once you have gotten the hang of using them.

Instagram is a very busy place and it has millions of users that are trying to do the same thing you are but instead of letting this fact discourage you let it encourage you. You can be successful on this platform as well. Many people receive a large audience on this platform, even if the starting is slow.

There are many people that you can lean on for help or you can look at competitions pages and see what they're doing differently with their photos and then learn from that and you can make your photos better as a result. There are many different tricks and there are many different helpful hints that we have gone over in this chapter to help you create engaging works so that people will stay with you instead of going to another profile or another page. By utilizing these tips for your benefit, you should guarantee that people are scrolling through your feed and your posts instead of others. Just remember that while it might take a little time, this is something that is very possible and you can do it if you are willing to put in the effort. You just have to remind yourself that you should not get discouraged if it does not happen within a week or a month. It will take time for people to find you but once they do, they will bring more people to you. In the next chapter, we will discuss the legalities that can become an issue with this social media platform and how to avoid it in the first place.

Chapter seven: Instagram Automations

Instagram Automations are what are known as bots and they are illegal to use. This is an important thing for people to know because they do not know that they are. Because they are illegal, this chapter will not only tell you the supposed benefits that people believe that they can get from using them but we will also tell you the negatives and to say that we are in no way telling you to use an Instagram bot or automation and in fact we are urging you not to because they are illegal.

When many people begin using Instagram they understand that it's a numbers game and because it's a numbers game, a lot of people began asking themselves if they should use a bot or an automation service to further their cause or further their profile and give them more followers than they can get themselves. It is harder than ever to be engaged following people on Instagram because it is not as easy as it used to be. Many people try to stay ahead of this problem and then turn to automated bots or automation tools to help them grow their audience.

If you are curious about these bots, we are going to list everything you need to know here. As it is illegal, this is not something that we would not recommend you do as we stated above. Instagram bots are designed to help you perform actions like commenting, following and liking other accounts through an automated service. These actions that most Instagram users do on a daily basis take up a chunk of your time but with the bots, you do not have to do anything because they will do it for you simply from you plugging in certain parameters that you want it to do for you.

Instagram bots are a little bit like eating an entire buffet. It might sound like a great decision, but deep down you know that it is bad and you know that you are doing something that is not right. This is where you need to worry. While they seem like a perfect solution, they are actually not. Any sort of automation on Instagram strictly violates the platform terms of use and Instagram bots can get your account banned or show banned.

Most Instagram bots access the API of Instagram without permission and this is clearly stated in the app's terms of use. This is a very strict violation. It also violates the API terms and platform policy. It is pretty common for users to see the positive effects of the Instagram bots on their accounts without looking at the repercussions until they get in trouble.

As it stands, a lot of the big names in Instagram automation are being shut down because it's not right and the users have started to notice that their images aren't showing up within their used hashtags as well and this has led to a massive decline in engagement with bots. There are multiple reasons why this could happen to your account but the main one is from using Instagram bots violating their terms of use. Many people do not recommend an Instagram bot because of all of these things.

Instead of using an Instagram bot, it is recommended that you do the work yourself or hire a virtual assistant, which is different. A virtual assistant is an actual person that can run your Instagram for you instead of relying on bots that are going to get your account shut down. Regardless of your stance on Instagram bots, what it really comes down to is whether you want to get in trouble and whether or not you want to be authentic. If you want to be authentic then you will have no problem attracting the type of people that you want to your profile. Instead of being caught up in the rat race of who can get the most followers the quickest, focus on getting people to notice the real you and getting real people to follow you for that.

Another reason you should not use bots? Instagram users can usually tell that these accounts are fake and they will be able to tell that you do not have real followers. They will have only a few followers and the bots also have incomplete bios and random pictures if they have any pictures at all. Most people think that bots are harmless. However, as close as just seven months ago, a very prominent newspaper was able to expose the massive business of buying and selling these fake followers on social media platforms and some of these bots actually use people's likenesses without their knowledge. They are employed to sway people's opinions or impact someone's influence online and they use these bots to scam other users because they think that they could be friends of theirs and they also scam unwitting users with a whole plethora of different methods. Buying them is cheap in most cases; depending on what you think is cheap. For example, $100 can get you a thousand followers or so. It is also very easy to do this and bots make ideal fake followers since they can follow a large number of accounts at once.

There is no shortage of finding these online. As early as two years ago people were able to determine that bots accounted for over 50% of all online traffic. Bad bots, however, which are the ones that are able to hack your password and carry viruses into your computer accounted for almost 30% of that.

The uncertainty of being followed by a bot outweighs any potential benefit and this is true even if the bots are benign. It is most likely connecting with you to make itself appear to be more realistic when it is not but many people use bots to attack people. The bots could befriend you usually through private messages of spam and phishing attempts and it is not easy to spot a bad bot from a good bot either.

Usually, however, you can tell that a bit is a bot when they have a brand new account with an incomplete profile or if they do not have very many connections. If something does not add up and you feel like something's wrong, you are probably dealing with a bot instead of an actual person. Instead of letting the bots follow you, you should report it to Instagram. There is no foolproof solution to getting rid of bots altogether. The best thing that we can do is report them and remember that using them is illegal and that they are trying to scam you while obtaining or trying to obtain harmful information about you.

Many also want to attach the files that you have on your computer so they give you viruses this is not a healthy way to gain followers as all your information can be used against you or for nefarious purposes. There are many other reasons why you should not use a bot and one of the biggest reasons is that they are unable to capture emotions or understand the concept of a photo. The only thing they can do is monitor what you are doing. For example, they only comment or add a comment that is based on hashtags. This would open up a large box of issues including the fact that you are opening yourself up to insensitive comments and trolling.

Another problem is when you are following thousands of accounts you will automatically have a very random feed and you will not be able to understand it. As you add more followers to your network, you can expect more and more random activity. If you do not care about your feed, you might not care about bots but if you are using Instagram and trying to gain actual followers that are going to stay with you this would be a problem because your feed is going to be a mess and you are going to have thousands of followers that are not real.

There is also no feeling as they are not humans and they do not replace human interaction. Many people understand that you are going to get less interaction on your feed. Along with this Instagram also has hourly limits and daily limits, which means that they monitor the number of activities and followers that you have. A typical user should not have more than a hundred and fifty likes or more than fifty comments every hour. Instagram also recognizes when your activity is unnatural and if you do not get shut down, your content will be invisible to followers or non-followers. This means that no matter what tags you are using for your posts no one will be able to see where you are posting.

There are many reasons that people think that a bot is a good thing and that it will help you and that is because of the features that the Instagram bots offer you. If you have a bot, it will delete posts for you and it will offer you the ability to unfollow people along with it being able to give you an auto-follow or follow back as well as being able to give you an auto comment. It is believed by many and it has been proven true, that Instagram bots can bring a serious danger to your Instagram account.

The Instagram automation who intrude on your social media platforms is the reason that they are banned in the first place. Along with violating Instagram's rules. The rules of that violation are not permitted on any of the popular social media platforms, which is why Instagram is not the only one that does not allow you to do this.

Another problem that many Instagram users face is that they are trying to use several automation tools on the same account at the same time. This is also illegal and will violate Instagram's terms of use. There are hundreds of different automation tools being used every day and they are presenting a variety of services that seem to be great for your account. However, even the most technologically advanced sources have proven that they are not safe and that they can harm the growth of your feed as well as the growth of your network and the growth of your Instagram account. Along with being banned or shut down, you need to make sure that you are doing the work yourself instead because then you are not violating any conditions and your security information is safe. There are much better ways to grow your Instagram that aren't going to be negative for you and an added plus is that you won't have your information used in a negative light and will keep you safe.

These bots are also very unpredictable when you are getting started and there are many times that a bot will comment on posts poorly and very inappropriately. A bot will comment on things at bad times. For example, a bot will comment on inappropriate things on posts about people who have died or people were going through a rough time.

To truly have a bot be beneficial would be an incredible hardship because the bots are always taking time to improve because they are not effective. You should also be aware that Instagram automation is not a complete solution to being an influencer or being able to succeed on Instagram. Automation engagement will only take you so far and it is not a substitute for content. All in all, it is widely agreed that if you're going to get followers on Instagram, automation and bots are not the way to do it and you should put in the time and effort yourself to make sure that you're doing the best job that you can. Being authentic and real at the same time is what will get the followers to come to you. Automation can only take you so far and it is not worth the legal ramifications or Instagram punishing you for using them.

Chapter eight: Turning Your Followers Into Dollars

When you are using Instagram and you are trying to turn your followers into dollars then you know that there are steps you will need to take to make this happen. Followers are an important part of Instagram but another important part of this is realizing how to use them to your benefit. In today's society, everyone is looking for extra income and it is becoming a necessity to do so. As such, people have been learning new ways to find extra income and Instagram is a wonderful way to do this but it takes some work. However, there are many different ways that you can get a lot of benefits and income from this platform.

The first thing that you should remember when you have your followers is to remember that if you build a relationship with your audience because this is going to convert your followers into dollars, which is what we are trying to do here. You should make sure that you are doing your research and see what it is your followers like and what they need. This may sound like something that you would not need but it is and this is important because it lets you develop a personal relationship with your followers. This lets them feel a personal bond or connection with you and this helps them feel closer to you. When they do this, they want to follow you because they feel like they know you. This also helps you understand their needs and what you can do to make them want to stay with you on your account.

This is an important thing for you to understand because it is important to gain followers but it is just as important to be able to keep them. It is great to be able to gain them because that is the first step but if you cannot keep them, you will not be able to turn it into money. This is going to be a problem for you because you are trying to make your Instagram a moneymaker for you as well.

Being loyal is another part of this. Post often. This is a big part of this as well. If you are unable to post every day this is understandable because life happens and emergencies happen as well. If you can try to make it at least once a week with your posts. Your followers will know that you do this and they will look for you and wait to see you. If you need time away simply, let them know and tell them you cannot wait to get back online. This shows them that they have a connection with you and that you are acknowledging it and respecting it at the same time.

Another way to let your followers know they matter? Show you care. Comment back to them and show them that you are taking the time to read what they have to say and that you care about them. This lets them feel more personal with you. Like a friend instead of just some random person on the internet. If you are able to show them that you care about them in a genuine sense, not someone who is pretending, you will find that they will stay with you and not leave for another account.

Everyone likes deals and they love to feel special as well. Many Instagram accounts are popular because they make their followers feel special and being able to offer exclusive deals for those same followers will keep them coming back repeatedly and this has been proven in many different accounts across social media. You still do not have to be complicated. In fact, if you keep them simple and fun it is a lot easier for them and it is a lot easier for you. For example, there are many book authors on Instagram that offers a free copy of their book, exclusive specials that go with their books such as a pin or a signed page, or even a personalized note from the author and all they have to do is follow directions. All they have to do in most cases is follow the account holding the giveaway and leave a comment below and then tag your friends and they get thousands of new followers and thousands of people trying to scramble to get their free item. This is a very good way to gain new people on your account. You could start a deal and keep your followers coming back the same way.

You can also treat your followers with a little special attention. For instance, if you are doing a live chat, you could invite all of your followers to live chat with you and answer questions for them. Let them know that it will be over within a certain amount of time and then you have created a situation where they get to actually talk to you and feel closer to you. This means that they feel like they matter to you and that they're important to you but it also shows that you care about your followers and that you're doing everything you can to make sure that they are staying with you. You are showing loyalty to them and then they, in turn, will show loyalty to you.

Everyone loves to feel special and this is why sending a personalized note or a personalized message is so important. Try not to just say something like I'm excited that you're doing this or this, instead say something like that appeals to them and something that would connect more with them to show that you were paying attention to what they care about and what they need. It can be tempting to promote your business in every post but you cannot stop engaging and providing good content for your followers. Make sure that you have a healthy balance between the two and make sure that you are not doing one over the other so that it does not get too overwhelming or annoying for your fans. This is important because if you are promoting your business more than anything else, chances are your fans are going to get annoyed and you might end up actually losing followers, but if you have a healthy balance between the two, they'll stay interested and they will keep with you.

Promote your followers as well. This is a great way to give back and gain credibility. Pick a day of the week if you choose to and pick a follower that you engage with and then share why you find them so amazing. You could even take it a step further and be the first to comment on why they are a fan of the week and how connecting with fans can be beneficial to the rest of your followers. Share your expertise with them and let them know that you know what you are talking about.

Testimonials are really big and you should take note of the positive things that your clients and customers are saying about you. You can take a huge sense of knowledge from what they are saying. Pay attention to what your followers are saying that they love about you. Sharing testimonials and understanding what it is that your followers love about you remind you of what you can offer them. More than that though, it provides them with the knowledge that they like you for a specific reason and you for that same reason meaning that you are learning the content they want to see because it is what they like about you. It is so much easier to gain followers once you figure out why it is the following you in the first place.

Another great tip that you can take advantage of is value. This tie into everything we have said above because the value is going to help that connection and how people see what you are all about. You should also know what sets you apart from the others in the same field you are in. Let us use the example of you using your Instagram for health and fitness. This is an amazingly popular niche on this app. Therefore, it could be easy for you to get lost among the crowd. You need to avoid this. What sets you apart from the others in that same category? This is something that you need to know because when you do, you convey it to your followers. Then they will see what makes you different. Another tip that can help with this is to know that you can add some value to your bio as well. Tell the people flocking to your page why they should be flocking to you and then following you.

When you post your content, remember your selling proposition. This means the one idea that makes you different and when you are posting to your account, you should be remembering to post your content around that idea. You have value in your content, you deserve to have people see it, and you deserve to make money off it. Share your account with the world and let them see that amazing content.

If you decide to use ads remember to make those about your followers or your audience but not to make them about you. Remember that you need to focus on what they need. Most brands that are out there focus on their own needs instead of the needs of the client. The important thing is that you need to remember that you will need to focus your attention on them and their needs.

Being able to focus on that idea around what you are trying to sell or what you are trying to show the people that are following you is going to help you let them understand that you are talking to them but you are not just trying to sell them things. You are trying to establish a relationship with them that will last. You can also ask questions and have conversations that revolve around the big idea that you have for your profile and your account. Build that trust and let them know that you are looking for relationships not sales. You will be able to get sales later but remember in the beginning you are just trying to get people to follow you.

If you like being controversial, you can be controversial. The most successful brands out there right now have fans as well as big people behind them. Your goal for your posts is to track your prospects and do not stay with everybody else that you do not want. Remember also, you need to be authentic as well. Stop trying to be someone that you are not and instead be real with your audience. You can be different. Different is a great way to stand out. It will let people relate more to people. This because they believe that you are authentic. Being real with your fans could be something as simple as letting them in a little bit on your life. People want to do business with people they know and trust. People want to follow people they know and trust as well.

You also need to focus on the transformation. This is an important part of this and you need to remember it. Your competitors are always focusing on their products and what they can offer people. If you are more advanced than they are, people are going to focus on your benefits and not theirs instead. You need to be advanced and focus on how these benefits are going to impact the lives of the people that are following you. They want to know how working with you or following you is going to be exactly what they are looking for to make them happy and they will want to stay with you and not another person that cannot do that.

When you are on social media, you need to remember that we live in a society that loves and is in love with Instagram. People want to see a clear benefit. They do not buy a product or service, they also buy experience and customer service. They are not just buying what you can do but they are buying how you can help them and treat them. If you do not take the time to share one piece of content that expresses your benefit then you are competition is more than likely to win the battle instead of you. You need to use your social media to articulate your solution and experience that you are going to be using with your audience.

You are going to be offering them benefits that other companies cannot and a great way to do this is to remember that you can share stories about past customers and how you were able to help them. This, in turn, would allow the new customers to identify with how you benefit them and know how you are going to benefit them in the future. You can also use social media to articulate what it is that you offer people. For example, if you own a pet store they are not just coming in to buy dog food, because they can get that anywhere. It is not just food that they are looking for they need to know how your store can benefit them in ways that other people cannot.

Bad habits are horrible and they could end up ruining your chances to be successful. A good example is procrastination. If you find yourself scrolling through Facebook, Twitter or other places like that or if you watch television and you're finding that you're getting too caught up, plan twenty minutes and name a specific time block at the end of your day as well and you'll be able to monitor your social media and respond to questions and engage in situations with the people so that they know that you're fully engaged.

You also need to evaluate your sales process. Is your content proactive or reactive? To make it productive and proactive make sure that your sales are flowing. You are going to need a calendar and map out your content ahead of time so that it will help you stay organized and on track throughout your workday. Most importantly, it is going to keep those people engaged by preventing your content from getting stagnant.

Remember whom it is you are writing for. If somebody asked you whom you are writing, for what would you say? You need to do homework by reaching out to your current followers and asking them what it is that they like to see but you can ask those questions about themselves as well so that they need to answer them for you. This is going to let them give you the information that you need and it will help you understand if there is something that you are doing that they do not want to see. If there's something that you're doing that they do want to see more of, being engaged with your audience is the best way to understand what it is that they're looking for because all you have to do is ask them and listen to what they tell you.

You should start looking at data. If you look, at it on your social media networks, it would be able to tell what quality brands are or the data that you need to know to get yours where it needs to be. Data was not created because numbers are pretty. In fact, it is the opposite. It is there to help you understand if you are falling behind or if you need to be working harder. If you want to increase the number of people that are following you and watching you through social media, then you need to dig into those analytics. Data provides brutal facts and you can make good decisions when you understand how to work with that data. The information can be adjusted to suit you better and you can work on your content strategy and how you are positioning the content that you are posting on your Instagram as well as the timing and the length of your posts. All of these things are going to make that data tip in the positive for you instead of in the negative for you. Most importantly, the tips and tricks that we have listed here are going to be able to help you gain followers, keep all the followers that you need and make sure that you are turning them into dollars. This will ensure that you are more successful with your endeavors on Instagram.

Conclusion

When you hear the word Instagram, you are probably thinking of beautiful pictures and great captions to go with them. You may also be aware of the fact that people are being paid to take pictures on this app and can make a fortune from doing so. Many have made this happen and it is becoming easier and easier to do this. Instagram is a wonderful place to be able to express yourself and get people to notice you in the way you want them to while making sure you are putting out quality content.

For many people, they do not understand just what Instagram can do for you and how you can use it for your benefit. It is not overly complicated to use and it can put you in touch with many different opportunities as not just an influencer but as a business owner as well. Essentially, you can consider Instagram to be a job. Even if you are an influencer, this is still going to be a job for you. You have to post and be informed, gain and keep followers, plan giveaways while making connections with companies and people and more. This is a big responsibility and it is most certainly a job because if you do not take it seriously, it will not work.

This sounds like something so simple but as we have said in this book, it really is something that you have to think about and take a lot of time to do. Instagram may be easy to use but if you want to be successful, it is something that you will need to put your effort into so that you can make it a success for yourself. We go over this in this book so that you will know what you are getting into and how to make sure that you are staying relevant.

We also explain the importance of your name and choosing the right one for you that will be able to take your Instagram to the next level. We do not just offer a single tip for this either, we give you as much information as possible so that you will be able to choose the best name for yourself. You should establish a niche as well and we also tell you how it is possible to do this in a way that is both engaging and fun. Remember, when you are looking for your niche you need to be thinking about what it that is you like and care about. This is not the only thing that goes into it but it will help you think about why you are wanting to utilize Instagram. If your fitness or health person, you will want to be connecting with companies or people that are along that same line. That would be your niche. Health and fitness. Likewise, if you are a fan of makeup and beauty, chances are that the best niche for you would be looking into being a beauty influencer or if you are a business owner, you are probably making your own or something that has to do with beauty.

The best way to get yourself noticed is to create great content that they want to see and remember that you should be posting on a daily basis while making sure that you are being influential as well. The tips that we have given you in this book just like these are going to be able to take your content and help you understand what your fans want to see and the type of content it is that you are wanting to post.

Instagram automation is another thing that people struggle with understanding mainly because they do not know what Instagram automation is. We explain the legalities of what this means and explain why you should not do this and how it can actually harm your account and the people following you. There are really good reasons that you should not use automation, we go over this thoroughly so that you know all of the information you need, and you can make sure you are not doing anything wrong.

Another reason that this book is beneficial to you is that we have taken the time to let you know what is illegal and what is legal within the parameters of Instagram. This is an important thing to know because it's not just the automation that is illegal it's other aspects that are illegal as well and you can face the danger of copyright infringement or you could get sued by another user. There is many legalities that go in with using social media platforms these days and we go over them so that you can have the best information possible and you can avoid beginners' mistakes. No one wants to have to deal with these issues if you don't have to and by following the tips and tricks that we've offered you in this book you can avoid them for yourself to make sure that you are not making those mistakes either. This will save you from unneeded frustration and it will keep your Instagram account from being banned. A great example that we used in the books is to find photos that are royalty-free. You cannot just download a picture from Google and use it. That picture belongs to someone and as such, you cannot use it legally. This can get many users in trouble and they do not even realize that this is something serious. To counter this, we have made sure to give you all of the information possible about it so that you do not fall into that trap as well.

The best part of the tips in this book is that when you follow the tips and you begin to use them for your benefit, you will notice that this gets easier over time. When you start with Instagram, it is going to be a job like the one we have said but it will get a bit easier once you are more aware of what you are doing and the process you need to go through for your followers and your content. Never forget though, this is still a job. While it gets easier in some aspects, it may be harder in others. Such as if you're doing videos and stories to get people to see you, you may not be able to do those as easily as pictures or vice versa so you'll need to be able to get your skills more into place and then practice them to get better with them as well.

Utilizing the information in this book should be able to help you create a great Instagram account with content that you will be happy with and your followers will be happy with as well. Instagram is a wonderful place to express yourself and have fun, but one thing that you will need to remember is that the way you present yourself to your followers is important. Maintain a good reputation and make sure that they are seeing you that you want them to see. Do not give them a reason not to like you. A great example would be if your account says that you are a vegan, you eating a double bacon cheeseburger in your pictures is going to make them unfollow you or be upset. This is going to change their perception of you and your reputation would be damaged. Instead, make sure that you are giving them a good view of who you are while being true to yourself. Doing this is so important because being true to yourself is what it is all about. If you are able to do this, your page will get the recognition that it needs and that it deserves.

www.ingramcontent.com/pod-product-compliance
Lightning Source LLC
Chambersburg PA
CBHW021441210526
45463CB00002B/598